Chasing
Digital

Chasing
Digital

A Playbook for the
New Economy

Anthony Stevens and Louis Strauss

WILEY

First published in 2018 by John Wiley & Sons Australia, Ltd
42 McDougall St, Milton Qld 4064
Office also in Melbourne

Typeset in 12.5/14.5pt Arno Pro

© John Wiley & Sons Australia, Ltd 2018

The moral rights of the authors have been asserted

A catalogue record for this book is available from the National Library of Australia

Cover design by Wiley

Printed in Singapore by C.O.S. Printers Pte Ltd

10 9 8 7 6 5 4 3 2 1

Disclaimer

The material in this publication is of the nature of general comment only, and does not represent professional advice. It is not intended to provide specific guidance for particular circumstances and it should not be relied on as the basis for any decision to take action or not take action on any matter which it covers. Readers should obtain professional advice where appropriate, before making any such decision. To the maximum extent permitted by law, the authors and publisher disclaim all responsibility and liability to any person, arising directly or indirectly from any person taking or not taking action based on the information in this publication.

Contents

Preface

To write a book collaboratively is a great opportunity to share, learn and find opportunities to lead. It is also, we believe, an avenue of service by which we can make our vocation accessible and useful to the broader community. We hope this book will be of interest to a range of readers seeking to understand the defining features of digital and the reasons for its unprecedented economic impact. Before thanking the many people who helped us with this book, we thought readers would be interested to learn a little about the background to this collaboration.

A NOTE FROM ANTHONY

For more than 25 years, I have been thinking about the application of technology and the internet to business. I have written extensively and had the opportunity to talk and work with a number of talented executives and thought leaders around the world. Over my career I have spent most time at the intersection of leadership, technology and strategy — domains I am deeply passionate about. These experiences are the foundation and impetus for this book, in which we apply well-tested concepts and strategy to the process of change through digital transformation.

I have had the great opportunity to work intensively with Louis, a friend, colleague and immensely talented future leader. *Chasing Digital* would not have been possible without his talent for communicating complex ideas, enthusiasm and commitment to this unique project.

A NOTE FROM LOUIS

My interest in business and technology blossomed during my time in Europe, where I worked with a handful of start-ups and met a number of different individuals who encouraged me to think deeply about the future of business and our economy. Having now worked in both start-ups and traditional incumbents, I'm excited about the opportunities and challenges that both types of organisations face. Like many of my generation, I believe that the most successful companies of the future will be those that not only disrupt markets but also strive to positively impact the communities they seek to serve. For those who wish to be successful in the digital age and beyond, the journey won't be easy, but the potential is huge and exciting. This book is about helping traditional incumbents unlock that potential.

Working with Anthony has been a fantastic experience, and his deep thinking and unique perspective have been fundamental to shaping my own thoughts on business and technology.

AS CO-AUTHORS

This book was born during an animated conversation between the authors in an office tower overlooking the skyline of Melbourne, Australia. We were perched in a prime spot, with a view up Collins Street towards the city centre — front-row seats to the bustling activity on many downtown construction sites. Melbourne is among the world's fastest growing cities, and it seemed as though new skyscrapers were rising every day, emblazoned with logos of companies that didn't exist five or ten years ago.

As professionals, we work with bold leaders, seasoned experts and powerful executives who want to tap into the opportunities being created by digital; their companies' names are also dotted across the city. But, we wondered, which ones would still embellish the urban landscape in another 10, or 50, years' time? And what types of businesses would take the places of those that disappeared?

By the end of our debate, we had agreed that, however uncertain the future, the indicators for success in digital were starting to become clear. There were unmistakable differences in strategy, mindset and structure between companies transforming for digital and those stalling in the face of changing economic forces. Our experience offered us rich evidence of what foundations are required and what steps are necessary for the leader who seeks to revolutionise an outmoded business model. We knew there were plenty of ideas on the subject floating around among consultants, and business magazines offered snippets of advice, but we believed there was no readily available guidebook for successful digital transformation.

Chasing Digital is that guidebook.

Acknowledgements

We have been fortunate to have had the help of a large number of people while writing this book. The following list acknowledges the many individuals, friends and colleagues who supported us throughout.

We extend our warmest thanks to Mark Briffa, Philip Colligan, Dave D'Aprano, Mark De Ambrosis, Alline Dos Santos, Anthony Ferrier, Kate Huckson, Wayne Jenkins, Sunil JNV, Shariq Khwaja, Steve Nola, Simon Overend, David Prakash, Jothi Rengarajan, Greg Rudakov, John Shin, Jodyne Speyer, Gowri Subramanian, Richard Susskind, James Turner, Tricia Wang and Steven Worrall.

Thank you also to Kath Walters for your superb coaching and editing.

To Bernard Salt, thank you for your inspiration, insights and advice on what it takes to write a book.

To Matthew Herring, David Linke and Emily Ulcoq, thank you for your support, feedback, encouragement and friendship.

Sarah Overton and Gennevieve Stokes deserve the largest thank-you of all. Your detailed analysis and critique were invaluable.

To my (Anthony's) wife Tiffany, my son Ned and my daughter Claudia, thank you for your belief in me. My love and support always.

To my (Louis's) family and friends who continue to support me, thank you.

Anthony Stevens
Louis Strauss
Melbourne, Australia
April 2018

Introduction:
The Fourth Revolution

A major change is underway in the business world. We are at the start of a new economy based on information, which some call the Fourth Revolution.

Here is how Klaus Schwab, founder and executive chairman of the World Economic Forum, puts it:

> The First Industrial Revolution used water and steam power to mechanise production. The Second used electric power to create mass production. The Third used electronics and information technology to automate production. Now a Fourth Industrial Revolution is building on the Third, the digital revolution that has been occurring since the middle of the last century. It is characterised by a fusion of technologies that is blurring the lines between the physical, digital, and biological spheres.

However you define it, the rate at which our new economy is transforming itself is incredible. Bio-engineering, particle physics, space technology, nanotechnology, autonomous vehicles, artificial intelligence and blockchain are just some of the most innovative technologies in the world today. Each revolution has advanced the human race further and faster than the last, and the new revolution is no exception. In fact, the speed of change it has brought has an exponential trajectory, and those who find themselves falling behind will find it harder and harder to catch up to the pacesetters. Nowhere is this more evident than in the business sector.

Every day a new book, blog post or article highlights the dramatic impact digital is having on businesses. There's talk of robots taking over jobs, of the mass of data that will drive decisions big and small, and of the impact of artificial intelligence on new business models and industries. Businesses around the world are struggling with the rapidly changing market, and new forces at play may threaten their survival in the short to medium term.

As a pre-digital leader, suddenly you find yourself on the back foot. The underlying business models you've helped create face disruption from digitally born companies that now dominate these markets. Through new business models designed for the digital era, these digital companies have managed to capture the hearts and wallets of modern customers, drastically altering their expectations, needs and wants. As a business leader of the old guard, you have entered a chase.

As the title of our book implies, we don't think the 'chase' is an altogether bad thing. The very fact you are on the hunt for something new primes you for a great leap forward, and your track record shows you are very capable of learning and implementing a successful new strategy. But the rate of technology change can be devastating to organisations that are not moving fast enough. Many companies ignore the danger until it is too late. Some discount the change out of arrogance, others are oblivious to it, while most simply don't understand it. As an experienced business leader, you know your company's future lies in disrupting your own business model, but you have not yet found a way to do this. If you put in place sound foundations, digital enablers and proven accelerators, your chase may well catapult your business to a new level.

Why this book, and why now?

The tools and processes you successfully applied in the pre-digital era no longer seem to have the effect they once did. In many circumstances, you find your organisation's growth stagnating or even declining. You are seeking answers. We know this because we work with leaders like you all the time. They are our clients and sometimes our colleagues. They are discerning enough to know that the basis of their current business model, their way of competing and their expectations of consumer behaviour are embedded in the pre-digital status quo. Typically, we find them looking for answers in all the wrong places. Our aim in writing this book is to focus your thinking and provide a practical guide to the essential principles you need to understand to pursue a future-focused transformation and chase digital.

A step-by-step guide to digital transformation

This book is for leaders who understand the need for digital transformation and are looking for a guide to lead their companies into a successful digital future before it's too late. We call these companies *pre-digital incumbents*.

Pre-digital incumbents have three defining characteristics:

- » They use business rules and strategies designed before the internet and the digital boom.
- » Technology supports the company's business model but is not what the company sells.
- » They are led by an executive team and governed by a board.

Pre-digital incumbents as a cohort have one major competitor: *big tech*. We define big tech by these characteristics:

» They have embraced and established new rules of strategy based on digital technology.

» They exercise financial and market dominance, redefining entire industries in the process.

» They place technology and the new wave of digital (which we'll explain soon) at the heart of their business model. Examples include Apple, Alphabet Inc. (the parent company of Google), Uber, Netflix, Microsoft and Tesla.

As an executive or director of a pre-digital incumbent, you will be written off by the media and digitally born competitors as a relic. We take another view. We believe you have a bright future in the age of digital disruption. Here's why:

» You were a dynamic and successful leader in the pre-digital world, and now you want to transition and embrace technology in a strategic and contemporary way.

» You want to shift technology from enabling support to centre stage of your business strategy.

» You have noted the rise of the new giants like Amazon, Alphabet Inc. and Alibaba, and you recognise there is much to learn and adapt from these companies.

» You are looking for practical ways to prioritise and manage your company's digital transformation.

» You want to learn and are curious about the ways in which technology is shaping your industry and creating opportunities for growth.

So what will this book give you?

As a step-by-step guide to digital transformation, this book is aimed specifically at leaders of pre-digital incumbents. You stand on the brink of enormous potential change. If you place digital at the centre of your company's strategy, organisational design and culture, it will become the self-sustaining economic engine of your business. The first-mover advantage is real, especially in the digital age, and you have the choice now to become a fast follower or accept the consequences of being a market laggard. In this book, you will discover what many of your competitors do not yet know. You and your business will be empowered by what you learn here. This book contains everything you need to understand to accelerate the process of digital transformation and secure your company's future.

Creating a long-lasting legacy

The idea of legacy resonates for us personally. One of the primary reasons we decided to write this book together was because of our 15-year age difference. We believe that this multi-generational perspective is integral to our understanding of the challenges you face today, as well as the challenges you'll face tomorrow. We set out to bridge the gap between the present and the future. In doing so, we have created the Chasing Digital Three-Part Framework, which is designed to help you successfully lead your company's digital transformation, as well as inspire new business models built for the future.

We wrote *Chasing Digital* not only to help your company survive and prosper in a digital world, but to ensure you create a long-lasting legacy. Legacy is extremely important. Without it, there can be no future. *Chasing Digital* isn't just about fixing current problems; it's also about creating durable foundations for the rapidly advancing future. We have written this book to help you lead the next generation of leaders a prosperous and healthy company, so they in turn can create their own legacy.

The Chasing Digital Three-Part Framework

This book is divided into three parts.

PART I: THE BIG DECISIONS

In chapters 1 to 3, we identify the problems that are holding every pre-digital incumbent leader back. These problems manifest in strategy, organisational design and culture. We examine how your digital future is intertwined with these three business fundamentals, and show why you must establish the right foundations to successfully transform your organisation.

PART II: DIGITAL ENABLERS FOR TRANSFORMATION

In chapters 4 to 6, we identify the three key technologies that, as a leader, you must understand to develop current and future business models and strategies. They are data, platforms and systems of intelligence.

PART III: ACCELERATING CHANGE

All leaders are experts in managing change, so why are boards and executives losing confidence and investing in technology too late? How can leaders effectively manage technology risk while still ensuring company growth? In chapters 7 to 9, we break down three vital accelerators of digital transformation that aren't discussed properly or enough in boardrooms today. They are investment management, technology risk management, and advice for boards and directors.

As a leader of a pre-digital incumbent, it is time to embrace change. Now more than ever, technology will be either your greatest asset or your worst enemy. Investments in technology can no longer be seen as isolated, one-off actions. The digital revolution requires you to take a new approach, with technology, people and data working in harmony and continuously evolving together. The dynamism within the new economy will only continue. We see no end to this change — it's a constant chase. With that in mind, let us show you how to *chase digital*.

Part I
The big decisions

At this point there are two important questions you need to ask yourself: what business are you in, and how do you make money?

As a leader of a pre-digital incumbent, you need to start by assessing the mechanical heart of your business — its driving economic engine — and what strategies will most effectively power it forward in today's new economy. In the past, you initiated your economic engine by identifying a niche, understanding specific regulations, accessing resources or taking advantage of a growth opportunity. When cultivating growth in your business, you assumed that these conditions didn't fundamentally change. Or if they did, it was a slow change, and your opportunity (and challenge) came from optimising your position in the resultant markets.

In recent years, new business models have been created that leverage the power of the internet — think Google, Facebook, Netflix and Amazon. This has led to a significant change in the economic engines and strategies that now power the world's most successful companies. Long-held assumptions about the fundamental drivers of high growth have changed. In summary, the internet has done two things pretty much in parallel: it has destabilised the basis on which an enterprise can succeed, and it has opened up entirely new ways of doing business.

The good news is that it is possible to move your business from one model to another. We recommend creating a new economic engine and running it alongside the old. This is by no means a small task, but with the right leadership, vision and personnel it can be done. That said, typically we see businesses trying to embrace digital, and implementing a new strategy, without changing two fundamental areas: organisational design and culture. *Organisational design* refers to the structure of your organisation and its position in the market. *Culture* is harder to define, but it is essentially the beliefs and habits shared by the employees of your company. Strategy, organisational design and culture are the critical components of the new economic engine you need to jump-start a successful digital transformation.

CHAPTER 1
Strategies for success

All men can see these tactics whereby I conquer, but what none can see is the strategy out of which victory is evolved.
Sun Tzu

How much of your current strategy will help you compete in the digital economy? And what have you done to adapt your strategy over the past few years? Perhaps you have acquired companies, expanded your services or products, or optimised your supply chain. You may have changed your organisation's structure a few times and appointed new leaders with fresh ideas. Perhaps you have met changing customer expectations by updating your website or refreshing your brand in some way. You also may have tried to increase margins by cutting operational expense lines.

Investment in technology and the appointment of new roles gives boards, shareholders and executives a sense that 'we are doing something'. But what most leaders have failed to do is align their newly implemented technology with their underlying business strategy and external market trends.

Many leaders talk about the need to promote a culture of innovation, make investments in start-ups, or invest in technology skills and experience at board and executive level. These individual moves are all worthwhile, but the critical thing is to link them together as a cohesive set of transformation initiatives. To do this you must think first about your business model, and what your customers want now and in the future, and align these fundamentals with the interests of shareholders. Internally, a new kind of strategy will require you to manage the process of change. Meanwhile, the competitive landscape, consumer preferences and technology are changing so quickly — and with such disruptive force — that putting in place a business strategy designed for our digital world is now a matter of survival.

Our solution is to go back to basics, revisit your economic engine and develop a new, digitally integrated strategy. That's the focus of this chapter. We will also show you how to implement that strategy, building on your current business and competitive advantage.

The old model

By now you are likely aware of the insufficient link between your strategy and technology. You see the symptoms everywhere. You make massive investments in IT, but these fail to make a significant impact on the bottom line. New competitors are taking market share.

Before we look at the solution, let's look at the problems in detail.

In 1980, Michael Porter published *Competitive Strategy*, which transformed the theory, practice and teaching of business strategy throughout the world. Porter's Five Forces framework (see figure 1.1), a model for analysing an industry to determine ideal corporate strategy, has been instrumental in defining the way leaders of pre-digital incumbents identify profitability and attractiveness. The model identified five features that play a part in shaping every market. At the centre is industry rivalry, which is enhanced by the bargaining power of suppliers, the threat of substitutes, the bargaining power of buyers and the threat of new entrants.

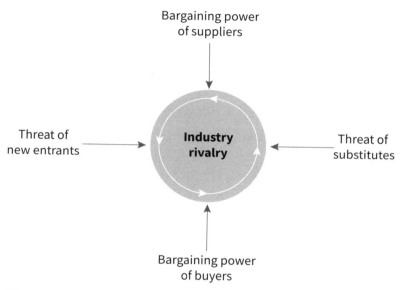

Figure 1.1: Porter's Five Forces

But the internet has changed everything, and the application of Porter's forces needs a refresh. In other words, a new approach to strategy and competitive advantage is needed.

The internet, social media, near-zero distribution and customer engagement costs, the explosion of data and platform-based business models, and the rise of artificial intelligence have forced speed and innovation to the top of the priorities stack for many boards and executives. These same factors have enabled unprecedented speed of transaction, globally scaled supply and distribution, faster time to market for new businesses, and heightened consumer awareness of what they are purchasing and the myriad alternatives. With a nod to Porter, figure 1.2 suggests what our new model of competitive forces in the digital world looks like.

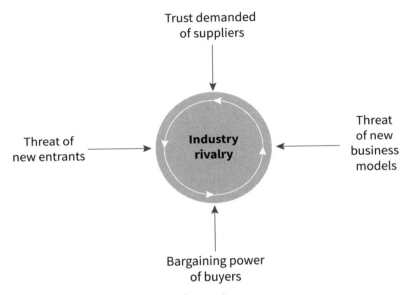

Figure 1.2: the competitive forces in our new economy

At its heart, our new economy is a customer's world, one in which buyers enjoy remarkable leverage, choice and influence. These forces can work against you. As a pre-digital incumbent, perhaps in the short term you will avoid the brunt of their impact while savvy new entrants capitalise on these forces to build market share in your category. Alternatively, you can learn to harness the momentum of digital, and use it to fuel your business growth.

One giant juggling act

Your company requires a dramatic change in strategy to respond to new market-shaping forces. You need to pivot your business model while at the same time making the most of your well-known brand and client relationships.

Unfortunately, you're up against some very well-funded start-ups. According to Crunchbase, as of the third quarter of 2017, both deal and dollar volume are at record highs since the dot-com bubble. With the number of venture funding rounds projected at 6146, and US$60.17 billion invested in that quarter, year-on-year this represented an increase of roughly 50 per cent. With this explosion in capital financing of start-ups, a compounding set of issues arise for larger businesses. The amount of money generally spent by a pre-digital incumbent to *transform* its business model into a digital business model reliant on data, software and platforms is a fraction of what start-ups invest in technology. Top talent is attracted by the wealth-creation opportunities and innovation culture of the start-up. Glassdoor.com, where employees can review and rate employers, has found for 2018 that all of the top-ranked small- to mid-sized companies in the United States and Europe were founded since 2002. Google held the number-one spot on *Forbes* magazine's Best Companies to Work For list in eight of the eleven years to 2017, due in part to the exuberance of its employees. (Says one: 'I love working for the greatest company in the history of the world! This place has been amazing and keeps getting better. There is nothing we can't accomplish and everyone walking the halls feels they can change the world.')

The bankrolled new models and cultural allure of start-ups are just the beginning of the many challenges you have to contend with. As we've seen with big tech, companies that invest in data, platforms and systems of intelligence will become more dominant. It follows, then, that those companies that own these capabilities are likely to be more successful. But what about those that don't? Will they survive?

Over the past decade, platforms of all shapes and sizes have started to change the nature of many industries. Whether you are in retail, manufacturing, business services, health or resources, you will have noticed that platforms play an increasing role in customers' buying habits and expectations. For example, for accountants there was traditionally a separation between the tool (the accounting system), its configuration, and the professional advice or accounting work itself. Over the past 10 years, however, accounting systems have moved online, making them easier and cheaper for customers to use, as well as giving the software provider access to a vast amount of customer data.

The forces of digital disruption are impacting the professional service industries along with most other industries. So what can you do about it? In order to move forward, there are two key concepts you need to understand. In his 1996 letter to shareholders of Berkshire Hathaway, professional investor and multi-billionaire Warren Buffett said: 'In business, I look for economic castles protected by unbreachable moats.' This quote highlights two ideas that are as pertinent to your new strategy in the digital age as they were when Berkshire Hathaway's stock was riding the mid-1990s economic boom:

1. **Your castle.** Your castle denotes the drivers of growth in your business — in short, how you make money. A little later we will show you how to apply demand- and supply-side economies of scale to digital platforms to retool the economic engine of your business.

2. **Your moat.** Your moat represents what is unique about your business and how this helps you take a sustaining and dominating — or, dare we say, monopolistic — position in the market. Your moat is essentially your competitive advantage. Soon we will show you how to re-examine this in the context of our new digital economy.

Along with a focus on your castle and moat, a successful strategy can be mapped into horizons of growth — each running in parallel and focused on a different term of the investment. For example, Mehrdad Baghai and Steve Coley's book *The Alchemy of Growth* provides a tool with three contemporaneous phases allowing companies to manage for future growth without killing their core products or services in the short term. Each horizon represents a time period over which you expect returns or a material impact on the financials of your business with the idea of investing in new products or services without impacting current performance.

The benefit of adopting a multi-horizon framework is in helping you to steer the change process within your company by quarantining execution into manageable chunks, allowing you to plan and manage the investments related to your strategy as it develops.

Reconstruct your castle

As a pre-digital incumbent, you know how you make money, right? The challenge you have is maintaining acceleration relative to the fast-moving digital economy. Trying to keep the current money machine working at the same time as pivoting makes you even more vulnerable to disruption. As you know, the internet provides a free, open and instant way to distribute products and services, and engage with your customers. This has forced a change in the traditional rules of business. So what powers your growth moving forward? We believe there are two areas you need to focus on:

» your value chain

» the demand-side and supply-side economies of scale.

VALUE CHAINS AND THE LAW OF CONSERVATION OF ATTRACTIVE PROFITS

In 2004, innovation expert Clayton Christensen wrote about the law of conservation of attractive profits. The premise of this law is that when profits decline at one point in the value chain, often due to commoditisation of an existing proprietary solution, a new opportunity for profit will emerge at an adjacent stage through the introduction of another solution.

This rule has been applied successfully and succinctly in describing the disruption of the taxi industry by Uber, the content and media production industry by Netflix, and the hotel industry by Airbnb.

Earlier we spoke about the professional services industry. The strategy that has been so profitable for professional services firms has been integrating human capital and intellectual property (IP). The professionals that attract the best people and have the best IP — and, in turn, the best reputations — are seen by clients as offering the most value. The final activity within the value chain is trusted deliverables. This is because the professional services are there to provide advice or some form of assurance. This advice or assurance comes in the form of a deliverable the client can then use. Furthermore, the deliverable is trusted, especially when provided from a top-tier or reputable firm.

It is also vital to understand the role data is playing. The pre-digital trusted deliverable is static and normally delivered in hard copy, such as slide decks and letters of advice, driven by thought leadership, much of it qualitative. Clients now expect quantifiable solutions backed by data. They demand dynamic deliverables that they can track and measure for themselves in real time. They also want solutions that help automate away low-value, highly repetitive jobs. Furthermore, IP shifts from pure knowledge, much of it qualitative, to proprietary data, which is both qualitative and quantitative. All of this means that proprietary data sets provide extremely valuable further differentiation. More on data in chapter 4.

Because software and the demand for data have fuelled the change in the professional services value chain, firms are prioritising investments in new technology and data sets. Granted, these purchases are coupled with human capital, but human capital has become easily attainable (commoditised) and less important when it comes to delivery, as new value (and profit) is found when a company's IP is hard coded into software solutions (deliverables) that leverage large and unique data sets. Figure 1.3 illustrates these changes.

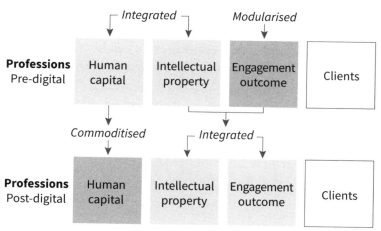

To date, the professions have integrated individual skill with domain-specfic IP, leading to varying levels of consistency in engagement outcomes. In the future, the IP and outcome will be integrated in a system providing clients with vastly greater levels of consistency at a lower cost.

Figure 1.3: value chain analysis — the professions

The critical point with this law is that you must spend time deconstructing your value chain and working through options to shift value creation by integrating or modularising different elements. Even if an alternative value chain seems unlikely or difficult to imagine, it is still worth considering as part of your strategy. No doubt there were plenty of early sceptics with Uber, Netflix and Airbnb. So rethink your value chain in the way we have done with the professions above. Can you see opportunities in your industry, and if not, why not? Is there a constraint or norm in the industry that you could consider further?

In all of the examples we've mentioned, the point of integration in the value chain moves to the right — closer to the buyer. This also aligns with one of the key moves big-tech companies make, which is to emphasise the demand side of your business. We'll discuss a number of benefits associated with this approach in detail in chapter 5.

DEMAND-SIDE AND SUPPLY-SIDE ECONOMIES OF SCALE

Traditional economies of scale inform a well-known strategy, which has likely helped you lower input costs on the supply side of your business. What you need to do now, though, relates to demand-side economies of scale. Demand-side economies of scale is where the value of a good or service increases as the number of users increases. The internet has profoundly accelerated the application of demand- and supply-side economies of scale by reducing distribution and marginal costs to near zero. This has created winner-takes-all markets, because once demand-side economies of scale are activated, growth can be exponential.

Some businesses create both supply-side and demand-side economies of scale, combined in a single customer proposition. This is called a platform, where demand- and supply-side forces accelerate the value of the platform itself, beyond the value of the company that creates the platform in the first place. The online retailer Amazon is the canonical example of this. In 2016, more than 100 000 small businesses across the globe achieved sales of more than US$100 000 through selling on Amazon. As of early 2017, Amazon Marketplace helps sellers reach more than 300 million active customers worldwide.

Amazon's primary driver is to offer the best experience possible, which attracts customers. It initially did this by offering a larger selection of books than any other store. As more customers buy from Amazon, third-party sellers are incentivised to sell through Amazon as this is where the customers are, creating more selection and thus more traffic flow to Amazon. This means that Amazon is able to more cost-effectively utilise its infrastructure, such as warehouses and distribution channels, which is the supply-side economies of scale aspect to Amazon's business model. This improved efficiency means Amazon is then able to reinvest these savings into improving infrastructure, which enables Amazon to lower its costs, as well as offer a better experience through enhanced delivery, meaning more customers. Customers also mean data, which helps Amazon further improve the user experience through better understanding its customers, allowing it to attract even more customers. So Amazon has created a virtuous cycle, referred to by tech blogger Sam Seely as the Amazon flywheel.

The supply-side economies of scale in this example are straightforward. A more efficient use of infrastructure brings down input costs and in turn lowers the price for customers. What is subtler in this model is the demand-side economies of scale, and the vital role the customer plays in furthering the virtuous cycle. In this feedback loop, customers fuel customer growth, which is why Amazon's primary focus is customer experience. Therefore, the more customers Amazon acquires, the more valuable its offering becomes. We'll explore this concept further in chapter 5.

APPLYING THESE STRATEGIES TO YOUR CASTLE

Again, when you consider the strategies for success for your business, think about your castle and moat. In relation to your castle, or how your business makes money, there are three strategies for success you can and should apply.

1. Rethink (and reconstruct) your value chain

Step back and examine the industry you are in, and work out where the points of integration and commoditisation are today. Draw a diagram of your current value chain; try to limit this to four or five value chain activities. Be careful not to construct this like a supply chain. Rather, focus on value. If in doubt, flick back to the professional services industry diagram (see figure 1.3).

Imagine a different world where the point of aggregation in your value chain shifts. To do this, decouple the integrated components into commodities, and consider what this would mean regarding the way you operate and your value proposition. The benefit of this approach is that you start to take into account a different makeup of your industry to help you better understand and manage disruptive threats.

2. Focus on the demand side of your business

Like most pre-digital incumbents, you have most likely focused on the supply side of your business to drive profitability and growth. Try flipping this emphasis to focus on your customers, their integration with your business, the data they create and the value they realise. Here are some ways in which you can do this:

» Map out the current and possible exchanges of data between you and your customer to determine where data can drive value. This concept is discussed in more detail in chapter 4.

» Consider the power of scale, and what additional benefits or services you could offer if you had a significant cohort of customers connected with you digitally.

» Identify complements, products and services you can provide to your customers with demand-side scale benefits.

There are three key benefits of this approach for your business:

1. You gather data about your customers' interactions with your business, which helps you hone your product and service offerings. This is discussed further in chapter 4.

2. A large customer base naturally attracts supply, either directly or through leveraging a marketplace of third-party sellers.

3. You can strengthen your core offering by complementing it with alternative products or services, further increasing demand.

3. Capture the momentum of the flywheel

Having reconstructed your value chain, and with a greater focus and understanding of the demand side of your business, you have created the operational components of a commercial flywheel. In mechanics, a flywheel is a device continually powered by its own rotational energy. In your enterprise, the flywheel is the virtuous cycle by which your realigned value chain — and both the demand- and supply-side economies of scale — make for a better, stronger value proposition, or a bigger flywheel. Just as a car's flywheel maintains the vehicle's momentum, so your business flywheel is designed to generate an ever-increasing amount of free cash flow. Free cash flow is calculated as operating cash flow minus capital expenditures. As some industries are more capital-intensive, you should ensure any comparison is done within your industry. The intrinsic benefit of free cash flow works with other elements of the flywheel to provide other natural points of competitive advantage — driving down operational costs, improving margins and strengthening the value proposition to your customers.

In part II, we will show you how the tools of the digital economy — data, platforms and systems of intelligence — provide revolutionary opportunities to harness the benefits of your flywheel. But first, let's discuss how to shore up your competitive advantage with an effective defence.

Widen your moat

Traditionally, moats have always protected castles. The wider the moat, the more defensible the castle. Swimming across a wide moat, besiegers were vulnerable to attack from above and to drowning. Conversely, a narrow moat offered defenders less protection. If a sufficient attacking force got over the water, they could gain access to the castle. As we explained earlier, the castle is your business, and the moat is your business's competitive advantage. The wider the moat, the more sustainable your competitive advantage.

So what does a strong moat in today's digital economy look like? What are the key ingredients? Though it may seem as if it is forever changing, our research indicates that there is an answer. Three forms of digital technology — data, platforms and systems of intelligence — are the key elements in the moats of the future. We have experimented with this idea, applying it to a wide range of industries and business models. So far, we have not found any industry where this isn't the case.

We'll discuss those elements in detail in later chapters. But first, it's important to recognise some of the elements that no longer make for a strong moat — at least not on their own.

FIVE MOAT FEATURES THAT NO LONGER DIFFERENTIATE

At the time of writing, we have identified some strategies that have been commoditised and do not help with the construction of your moat. They are critical building blocks to assemble digital capabilities for your business, so you cannot ignore them, but they are no longer differentiators:

1. **A great user experience.** This was once a barrier to entry, but not anymore. Creating an awesome user experience requires creativity and expertise. However, it is not enough to form your moat.

2. **Relying on scale and distribution.** For the professional services industry, limiting services to a particular location was standard practice, particularly among large law, accounting and audit firms. But investments in cloud computing made by the likes of Amazon, Microsoft and Google have changed the

game. Scale and distribution are now a commodity, not a competitive advantage.

3. **Using third-party software.** If you can buy it (either software as a service or on-premise), it's not that interesting. Third-party technology itself provides no competitive advantage; it is what you do with it that counts.

4. **Basic applications of artificial intelligence.** Ultimately, artificial intelligence (AI) is software that learns. Just as a child learns and becomes an adult, AI improves its intelligence over time. What's unique and sustainable is not that a child can learn, but what they learn and how they learn. The same applies to business. What makes an AI system unique — and provides a competitive advantage — is not the ability to learn, but *what* the system learns.

5. **Digital supply-side economies of scale.** The bigger you are, the more operating leverage you have, which lowers your costs. Software as a service (SaaS) and cloud services can have substantial economies of scale, meaning your revenue and customer base can scale while keeping your product the same. That said, digital supply-side economies of scale alone will not provide a competitive advantage, as anyone can access the same cloud infrastructure, tools and distribution channels.

Now that you're aware of some of the features that *won't* make for a strong moat, it's time to discuss some of the features that will. We'll start with traditional moats and then move on to digital moats.

THREE TRADITIONAL WINNING MOATS

It is important for a moat to provide a sustainable competitive advantage that cannot be easily replicated over time. Some of the greatest and most enduring technology companies are defended by deep and wide moats. For example, Microsoft, Google and Facebook all have moats built on demand-side economies of scale, network effects and a platform, which we will explain in more detail in chapter 5.

There are three traditional moats you need to consider in relation to your business. The application of each of these will vary depending on the nature of your industry, product and service:

1. **Proprietary software, technology or trade secrets.**
   Proprietary software or methods is where most technology companies start. These trade secrets can include novel solutions to hard technical problems, new inventions, new processes, new techniques and patents that protect the developed intellectual property. Over time, a company's IP may evolve from a specific engineering solution to accumulated operating knowledge, or insights into a problem or process.

2. **High switching costs.** Once a customer is using your product or service, you make it as difficult as possible for them to switch to a competitor. You build this stickiness through a lack of substitutes, coupling your product or service with other products or services, or integrating part of a crucial customer process. Any of these can act as a form of lock-in that will make it difficult for customers to leave.

3. **Brand and customer loyalty.** A strong brand can be a strong moat. Over time, with each positive interaction between your product or service and your customers, your brand advantage gets stronger. At the same time, brands are particularly vulnerable to matters of trust, and your brand strength can quickly evaporate if your customers lose trust. This risk is becoming even more acute as companies are more exposed to cybersecurity attacks, which can almost instantly bring a business to its knees.

In addition to traditional moats, there are strong digital moats you can emulate. This is where we return to the notion of the flywheel.

Digital moats: the flywheel revisited

Effective digital moats defend some of today's largest and most future-proofed companies, including Microsoft, Google and Facebook. These big-tech businesses are dominant precisely *because* of their dominance. In other words, they are using technology to harness and reinforce the self-perpetuating motion of demand-side economies of scale. They have become digital flywheels.

In part II, we will expand on the digital tools you need to employ in order to capture the value of a digital transformation strategy. However, it is important now to deconstruct the component parts of the flywheel, as each element adds depth to your digital moat. Remember, your product or service achieves demand-side economies of scale if each additional user accrues more value to every other user.

Demand-side economies of scale and the associated flywheel cannot be built overnight. There is a systematic, three-staged approach to creating this digital moat. As discussed earlier, the flywheel gets bigger when you bring supply-side economies of scale into the mix. Let's take a look at this process.

In phase 1 (see figure 1.4), you start by offering a differentiated product or service that creates a great customer experience, attracting customers. Customers fuel your company's growth, but they also create data, which can be used to improve your product or service. This further improves the user experience, attracting more customers and generating overall company growth. The flywheel has begun to spin.

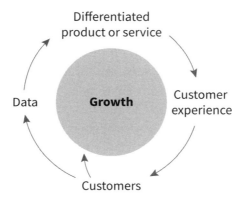

Figure 1.4: the flywheel growth strategy — phase 1

Source: Adapted from the Virtuous Cycle, as drawn by Amazon and adapted by Sam Seely.

In phase 2 (see figure 1.5, overleaf), it is all about increasing the 'spin'. After some time, your company will grow and you'll be able to invest in improving infrastructure. The goal here is to improve supply-side economies of scale, which in turn feed into bolstering the customer's experience, attracting more customers and driving growth.

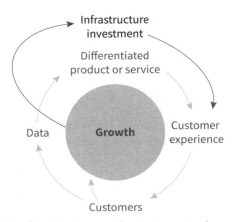

Figure 1.5: the flywheel growth strategy — phase 2

Source: Adapted from the Virtuous Cycle, as drawn by Amazon and adapted by Sam Seely.

In phase 3 (see figure 1.6), we introduce third parties into the mix. Third-party sellers offer products that complement and improve your product or service, enhancing the customer's experience, attracting more customers and fuelling growth. Third parties also increase the amount of data you can collect, which will further help you improve your offerings. We'll discuss third-party sellers in much more detail in chapter 5.

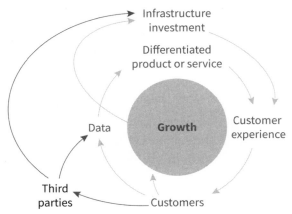

Figure 1.6: the flywheel growth strategy — phase 3

Source: Adapted from the Virtuous Cycle, as drawn by Amazon and adapted by Sam Seely.

Once in place, the flywheel fuels itself and is therefore self-perpetuating. It's a powerful beast. Both Apple and Amazon employ this model, which has been the backbone of their success. Again, we'll explore the concept of supply-side economies of scale in much greater detail in chapter 5. If you are then able to incorporate all or some of the non-digital moats — proprietary assets, high switching costs and loyalty — you suddenly have an extremely wide and defensible moat, which will provide your company, your employees and your customers with fantastic value well into the future. Generating and sustaining a higher volume of free cash flow is the most obvious sign of an effective economic moat. The key to balancing and profiting from all these strategic elements lies in an open-minded examination of the competitive forces in your industry, opportunities for shifts in the value chain and an evaluation of what your customer really wants from your business.

Questions

1. Does your strategy incorporate the effect of internet-related ease of distribution and the digital nature of our new economy?

2. Have you mapped out the value chain for your business and industry? Which activities that are currently integrated could be modularised?

3. Have you considered the nature of demand-side economies of scale and their application to your business and industry?

4. Can you envision fundamental shifts in your industry's value chain like the ones driven by Uber, Netflix and Airbnb?

5. What is the flywheel in your business or industry, and what does it look like?

6. Do you have confidence in the areas of competitive advantage for your business, or do they seem a little flimsy?

7. How digitally connected are you with your current and future customers?

8. If information asymmetries in your industry were reduced, what new opportunities and businesses would open up?

9. What provides you with a sustainable competitive advantage and the ability to command a premium over the competition?

Chapter summary

It is critical that you develop a strategy to compete in today's digital economy. Without it, any investment in technology will not work. Consider again the quote by Warren Buffett: 'In business, I look for economic castles protected by unbreachable moats.' Apply this to your business from two points of view — your castle as the economic engine, and your moat as your competitive advantage.

There are three strategies for your castle that you can and must apply, in this order:

1. Rethink the points of integration or commoditisation within your value chain. This will help you see and manage systemic and structural risk in your industry, and help protect your business from disruption.

2. Focus more explicitly on the demand side of your business. The benefits of doing this include the data you will have about your customers' interactions and preferences, a magnet to help hone the supply side of your business, and an easy way to position complementary products or services with your clients.

3. Create a flywheel (or virtuous cycle) stimulating ever-increasing free cash flow. This is a tremendous goal to work towards. It will force you to think through the economic impact of the supply and demand sides of your business, as well as what underpins your economic engine.

Keep in mind the moat features that no longer provide a point of difference:

» a great user experience

» relying on scale and distribution

» using third-party software

» basic applications of artificial intelligence

» digital supply-side economies of scale.

This is not to say these features are not valuable, but they are not enough to provide a sustainable competitive advantage — at least not on their own. There are, however, some winning moats and areas of competitive advantage you *should* consider as part of your business strategy, which we've broken down into traditional moats and digital moats.

These are the key takeaways in relation to your competitive advantage:

» Consider the role demand-side economies of scale can have in the defensibility of your business.

» Challenge the emphasis on moats that no longer provide a point of difference and, where possible, reduce investment in these areas.

In the next chapter, you will learn how to structure your business to allow you to set a new course and at the same time keep the current machine ticking over.

CHAPTER 2
Organisational design

Do not go where the path may lead, go instead where there is no path and leave a trail.
Ralph Waldo Emerson

As the model of your business, organisational design describes your company in terms of people, roles and structure. It is the blueprint for your organisation's capabilities and business strategy. Without revising the mechanics of your business, you cannot execute new strategy and implement the changes you've drawn from chapter 1. If you don't get the engineering right, you will end up with confused roles, a lack of internal coordination, siloed teams, variable outputs, ineffective decision making and stagnation. The most significant problem you'll face, though, is a lack of speed, as pre-digital incumbents aren't traditionally designed for the fast pace of our new economy.

Our dual-engine approach to organisational design will ensure your business is equipped to thrive in the years to come. The idea is to serve your current customers while in parallel building out the capabilities to meet the needs of your future customers, even if these sets of customers are the same. In this chapter, you'll discover how to transform your organisational design using a proven strategy called dual transformation. As part of this process, you'll become familiar with two additional key concepts, known as Engine A and Engine B.

When your primary engine runs out of fuel

In our new economy, pre-digital incumbents can find themselves bogged down by an outdated organisational design. They face slowing growth and decreasing market share. And as new competitors challenge traditional models, the tricks businesses used to drive growth no longer seem to provide a reprieve.

The issue becomes not just organisational design, but the nature of how you make investments to stimulate further growth. For the past few decades, pre-digital incumbents grew by entering a new market and innovating, taking an ever more sophisticated product or service to the same set of customers. As your organisation became more knowledgeable about its customers, it could better meet their needs. Clayton Christensen calls this sustaining innovation — a process of incremental change in which products or services become faster, cheaper or better. You will learn more about this in chapter 8.

The catch is that sustaining innovation isn't about constantly creating new markets. Organisations increase profits by serving customers more efficiently over time. Unfortunately, as businesses mature, their focus tends to move away from their customers' needs towards immediate revenue — a perspective shift from external to internal. Key performance indicators protect the status quo and, inevitably, resources move from innovation-based initiatives to those activities that deliver short-term results. In most businesses, decision hierarchies and steering committees are mechanisms commonly used to justify a proposed departure from normal investment. Yet, if constrained by the same metrics and mindset, decision makers and committees are either conservative in nature or slowed down by the need to be overly consultative to ensure and maintain support. This problem is exacerbated when delivery timelines and returns for new initiatives are longer than an annual profit cycle.

This approach works when things are moving slowly enough that any single external force — such as new technology, a slight change in the competition or even an economic downturn — can be pre-empted or reacted to before any serious damage is inflicted. But this is not the reality in our new digital economy because we now face a swath of entirely new ways of doing business built on a swath of new technologies. The billions of dollars tied up in the old growth models, infrastructure, workforce and intellectual property cannot address these new opportunities.

Of course, the immediate impact is not as evident. Kodak provides one very well-known example of this. Kodak was always the leader when it came to film cameras and was considered a highly innovative company. In fact, it was so innovative that it invented the digital camera in 1985. Yet it failed to embrace the new technology because it was firmly entrenched in the film, chemical and paper business. Any inroads it did attempt to make in technology were usually too tightly coupled with its film business, or were dismissed by leaders who saw digital as the enemy, rather than as an opportunity. In 1996, just before the digital camera revolution kicked in, Kodak reached its peak revenue of US$16 billion; in 2012, the company filed for bankruptcy. This calamitous fall from grace was due to Kodak's fear of change and fruitless attempts to protect the status quo.

The only way to overcome such resistance in the face of change is a complete organisational overhaul, a complex and costly endeavour for any large enterprise. The innovation machine for new markets must be lean, agile and responsive. Leaders of large companies are reluctant to take action without certainty of success. Sadly, history shows there is only one real guarantee: the longer your organisation protects the status quo, the lower your chance of survival becomes. A lean, agile and responsive business is one that, by its nature, embraces risk, yet your job as a leader is to reduce risk. So how can you achieve a smooth transformation given the realities of your current operating model?

The ultimate pivot

The word 'pivot' denotes a rapid change from one strategy to another, which quite often involves changing the business's original strategy, its target market and its pricing. Most pre-digital incumbents don't pivot, and perhaps don't even know how, because they have been focused on sustaining innovation, which in the past was a more than adequate approach.

The pivot is mainly about risk and reward. Those making the decisions recognise that to continue as they are will yield a lower likelihood of long-term success. When a start-up pivots, it effectively abandons everything to do with its past strategy and approach in favour of a new direction. It makes sense in this context as there isn't much for the start-up to lose, and keeping both strategies running in parallel would be an expensive distraction and would likely create confusion for prospective customers. But for an established business the pivot requires deeper consideration, as millions (or billions) of dollars in revenue and thousands of jobs may be at stake.

The question for the established business, then, is: how do we pivot? A successful pivot would, in the medium term, mean changing the nature of the product or service offered to meet new and emerging demands, while in the short term continuing to exploit current resources and investments. It becomes a juggling act of sorts that involves digitally optimising your existing economic engine so as to squeeze as much as possible out of it (we call this your Engine A), while building out your new economic growth engine to meet new demands (your Engine B).

Innovation consultant Scott Anthony calls this dual transformation. It is essential to make the distinction between your Engine A and Engine B, because monolithic transformation is simply too big a task when you're dealing with thousands of employees, expectant shareholders and legacy systems. This twofold approach has its own challenges and complexities, but will help you create an organisational design that remains relevant well into the digital future. In the following sections, we'll discuss the components of Engines A and B in more detail.

Engine A

Engine A is your current economic engine. Maximising longevity is the objective with Engine A, so it's essential to find more efficient ways to meet your customers' needs. Market demands, expectations and forces have changed in all markets, so if you want your core business to survive, it's imperative that you make the appropriate changes. This may sound obvious, but execution is tricky, and markets are riddled with stories of failure.

To ensure any changes you make are a resounding success, the first part of this journey is to understand why your current customers pay for your product or service. This will help you determine what your core competencies are and what you need to be focusing on to ensure the longevity of your Engine A.

Work on the basis that growth will come from taking market share from your competitors. To do this, you need to truly understand your customers' needs as well as their experience. To understand your customers, you need to take the time to talk to them and analyse their experience, whether through surveys, targeted interviews and focus groups or by observing how they interact with your offerings. The key is to work with them to uncover their pain points and desires. When you conduct this research, the customer needs to feel that working with you is as much in their interest as it is in yours. If they believe they are in partnership with you, then they will be much more willing to help, and will provide you with insights that would otherwise be impossible to unearth. Data analysis, which we will discuss further in chapter 4, will also play an integral role in further understanding your customers. This type of customer research will also be integral for your Engine B, so it isn't something that should be treated lightly.

Amassing data on your customers should be a primary focus, and you should make a point of collecting both qualitative and quantitative data. Centralising your data will also ensure you are able to elicit the best possible insights from the information, providing you with a holistic and complete customer profile. Having disparate data stores, on the other hand, leads to data being lost or forgotten, as management practices are typically inconsistent and in some cases non-existent. We go into more detail about how to set up and manage secure data in chapter 4. Finally, talk to your employees. They know the market and your customer better than anyone else. When undertaking this exercise of customer discovery, assume nothing, as biases can influence your findings dramatically.

Next, cut anything that isn't core to the value you provide to your current customer. A good way to assess whether or not a product or service is relevant to your customer and economic engine is to conduct a simple return on investment (ROI) analysis. Activities that have a direct impact on the bottom line can be ranked very easily, while soft benefits can be harder to quantify. That doesn't mean overall value cannot be ranked by those who understand your business model well. Just remember to ensure objectivity when assessing value — leave egos and attachments at the door. It may be worth engaging a consultant to help you with this exercise. Through conducting a thorough ROI and ranking analysis of all the initiatives within your organisation, you'll uncover a number of initiatives that do not contribute to the success of your Engine A and are thus money burners rather than earners.

Start with new initiatives that aren't closely coupled to your core offering, as well as new products or services that have been bolted onto your primary product or service. Is the value they are providing to the customer worth the investment? If not, then they need to be terminated. This process can be difficult, as different people will have different agendas and biases, which means strong leadership is required to objectively discontinue lacklustre initiatives.

Many of these new initiatives may actually be digital in nature. If that's the case, ask yourself whether these digital initiatives are centralised, or whether they are siloed and run completely independently of each other. Typically, disparate digital initiatives are underfunded, lack a proper development roadmap and use outdated technologies. Therefore, centralisation is imperative for the efficient development and management of your digital capabilities, and can significantly cut costs.

Look for bottlenecks and chokepoints too, as well as duplicated efforts and highly manual and repetitive processes. It's important to remember that your Engine A transformation is about being lean while ensuring your customers' experiences aren't negatively affected. Consolidation is the key here — cut the fat.

To do this, start by mapping out your as-is processes on a whiteboard, including all internal activities and customer touchpoints — the more detail the better. Though this can take some time, it's an extremely valuable process in helping you understand all aspects of your organisation and identify internal inefficiencies and chokepoints. Bring in people from all departments so you can create a truly detailed end-to-end workflow of your organisation — you'll be amazed at what you find. From here you can identify opportunities for cost cutting as well as areas to invest in, and in doing so design your ideal target state and create a systematic roadmap to achieve it.

By now you may be asking yourself whether the work done to ensure the longevity of your Engine A requires further investing in digital capabilities and technologies. The short answer is yes, but only if it leads to a reduction in overall spend. Historically, enterprise IT teams have been extremely costly because of outdated operating models and technologies, so engaging with them to help streamline your Engine A would be expensive. A viable alternative is to spin up a digital team that uses agile operating models and cloud technologies, and that works closely with your business units to help reduce costs through developing and implementing cloud-based solutions. These teams need not be large given that they do not require on-premise infrastructure. As already mentioned, make sure these digital initiatives are centralised to ensure they are optimally managed and that your data is also centralised and readily accessible.

Regardless of how you streamline your Engine A, always ask yourself whether the outcome will be cheaper than the status quo without negatively affecting what your primary customer values most.

Once you have initiated the streamlining of your Engine A, unlocking free cash flow, only then should you start thinking about your Engine B.

Engine B

Engine B is about creating new revenue streams. You do this by building a team that initially focuses on the discovery of these new areas of growth, which eventually take over as your primary economic engine.

The underpinning ambition of the Engine B team is to redefine how business is done within a specific market and to drive your business into new categories. Your team will need to adopt a real customer- and data-centric point of view. As explained in chapter 1, Engine B takes responsibility for spinning your flywheel as quickly as possible, and first-mover advantage is the key to locking in customers.

To achieve such an objective, you will need a team of resilient digital natives with a business mindset. Many of them will come from outside the organisation, which is critical because they won't be burdened by your company's old habits and thinking processes. That said, it's important to draw on expertise from the old business to help ensure alignment with the shared goal. Another option is to buy a start-up or small business innovating in a market sector that could leverage your assets or capabilities.

Engine B will focus on data, software and customers. It should run concurrently with your Engine A transformation, but this new team should in no way be bound by the shackles of your old business model. It must have complete autonomy to create new ways of doing business. It is also imperative that this new team take a digital-first approach, which means management must ensure they do not burden the team with habits, thinking and processes that are optimised for pre-digital markets.

In the rest of this section, we'll discuss four key ways to ensure the success of your Engine B.

SUPPORT AND EMPOWER YOUR ENGINE B TEAM

Your Engine B team should be independent. It would be foolish, however, not to have them leverage the capabilities, IP and resources of your core business. This involves determining what assets are used to provide a competitive advantage and unlock new revenue streams. It then becomes a bit of a balancing act between your Engine A and your Engine B — one that needs to favour Engine B. As a leader, you must ensure that your Engine B team has minimal dependencies. For instance, sharing human resources with other divisions within the organisation is a dependency, as a team focused on future growth is now awkwardly coupled to the legacy business through sharing resources. Such dependencies kill momentum, and momentum is critical for the success of this new team. So, if conflicts for resources arise between your new and old businesses, it is essential that your new engine receives priority. As the efforts of the new team begin to be validated and to scale, adequate resources from the old business need to be moved to the new business so it can continue to grow. Remember, the purpose of Engine B is to eventually become your primary economic engine, so make sure you give it the right fuel to get out of first gear.

While your Engine A transformation is focusing on cost-cutting and streamlining operations, this should in no way affect the team that is leading your Engine B. One of the trickier aspects of managing these two buckets is to ensure there is a shared organisational identity that is coupled to a common fate. They may operate in two very distinct ways, but they must share the same vision. This is extremely important because, without this common link, a chasm will form between your old business and your new team, which will, in turn, undermine the success of your Engine B, as well as any other change initiatives. You must avoid creating an 'us versus them' mentality, while still ensuring that Engine B receives priority. To achieve harmony between the two, it's imperative that your leadership team is structured accordingly. This means the two distinct divisions are led by the appropriate personnel: a transformation expert who understands digital for your Engine A, and a calculated risk taker who seeks out new opportunities for your Engine B. Though these two leaders will be focusing on two very different things, they must be able to come together with the other executives within the organisation, and must share a common vision and roadmap.

Internally, your Engine B team will be leading the charge into a brave new world. With no shackles, they are free to embrace digital fully. This means working in an agile fashion, leveraging cloud computing and dispensing entirely with costly IT infrastructure. The key here is to ensure that the team are free to hypothesise, test and fail. They should be experimenting with proving different concepts. Not every project will succeed, but the learning opportunities will be rich and plentiful. Each decision they make needs to be calculated, but uncertainty has to be embraced. Through early successes, the team will gain buy-in from the rest of the organisation, ensuring the momentum continues to build. As success grows, the team has to remain small and nimble, ensuring they have the flexibility to pivot as they continue to learn. From the lessons learned, the Engine B team will be able to identify the resources and skills they lack, which will help them define and map out the capabilities they need to achieve their goals. These lessons should also spill back into your core business to ensure these two engines can work together. It is important to remember that this new team must create a culture that embraces change and chaos, but operates and executes at an extremely high level, delivering outstanding results.

SOFTWARE MUST BE AT THE HEART OF ENGINE B

Software is changing how businesses operate as well as what customers value. Within any pre-digital incumbent, there is a plethora of opportunities just waiting to be digitised. Your Engine B transformation has to be radical, especially as competition, both new and old, aggressively reduces prices, redefining value within the market. To counter diminishing margins, you need to figure out how you can distribute what it is your customer values at a significantly lower cost and to more customers than you do today, while better meeting their needs through implementing new, digital operating models. This will also include looking to new opportunities that lie outside your immediate market and creating innovative solutions that provide entirely new forms of value. Doing so will require you to rethink your operating model and strategy, and a vital part of this will be the development of software. While your Engine A was entirely about streamlining the status quo, your Engine B isn't constrained by any legacy, so you are free to focus on new forms of value (beyond just value for money) for both current and potential customers.

Software allows your business to scale exponentially because digital distribution is practically free and ubiquitous. A retail assistant, no matter how good, can serve only so many customers at any one time. With software, there is no such limit. Scale depends simply on how well you can sell your product, as well as how receptive the market is to what you are selling. Furthermore, cloud computing ensures that software can be deployed and accessed almost anywhere in the world at the touch of a button. When you start introducing artificial intelligence into the mix, (more on artificial intelligence in chapter 6) your software begins to teach itself and make critical decisions without the need for human intervention.

Software has given rise to the as-a-service model, making it viable for customers to use goods on demand without having to pay for them outright and claim ownership. Examples of this are Microsoft Office 365 and Adobe Creative Cloud, which are cloud-based software solutions that customers pay for by subscription. Similarly, organisations can employ a utility model, which is fundamentally the same as the as-a-service model except that customers pay a subscription fee, say monthly, in addition to paying for the exact amount they use. The great thing about the utility model is that it creates customer lock-in yet still ensures customers pay only for what they use.

Your Engine B will require a new operating model. A fantastic indicator of whether you have sufficiently changed your operating model is if the metrics you use to measure success have changed. For instance, in the services industry, many repetitive processes can be automated using Microsoft Excel. Use of this software with customers can change the way you generate fee income — away from human-based hourly rates to software-based packages that are billed on an annual subscription. The benefit of this approach is that you can measure in real time things such as customer logins, page views and the time spent on each webpage. This type of information gives you direct feedback on how your customers are interacting with you, what they like and, of course, what they don't like, enabling you to react and make changes almost instantly.

In essence, software implementations allow you to create entirely new business models, deliver bespoke and novel solutions at scale, and better manage customer relationships and foster new ones. While your organisation adopts new software-based solutions, legacy divisions need to be supported and upskilled as they transition into your Engine B initiative, so their knowledge is not only retained but improved upon. Your Engine B delivery team therefore need to be more than just techies — they must have strong business skills and knowledge to support the business and strategy changes associated with implementing these new software-based solutions.

A DIGITAL, DATA-DRIVEN MINDSET IS KEY

Once you begin to create a digital ecosystem of software-based products and solutions, you start amassing a vast amount of data. Data will be vital to fuel your Engine B and, as previously discussed, will also play a significant role in your Engine

A transformation. We will go into more detail about data in chapter 4. At this stage, all you need to know is that using your data efficiently to provide insights into how you operate, your customers and the wider market is essential if you are to maintain a competitive advantage.

Pre-digital incumbents need to begin to operate in a way that ensures data is captured and utilised. Time and money need to be spent on creating a process and facility to store, manage and protect data. Data science and business intelligence tools that can be accessed and used by any team within the organisation must be layered above the data to provide insight and help drive strategy. Data needs to be able to flow freely between teams, and teams need to work together with respect to how they use data and make decisions. Accrued knowledge should be easily accessible. It is essential to put in place data management standards and processes that enforce best practice across the organisation, while also ensuring they are flexible enough to allow for creative data exploration.

Your Engine B team needs to be structured in a way that allows them to make critical decisions as data becomes available in real time. Data will be an important part of your digital moat; it's your enterprise rocket fuel, so it's vital that it takes centre stage. More on data and decision making later.

START ON THE DEMAND SIDE WITH THE CUSTOMER

Given that the cloud and the internet have wholly disrupted how goods and services are distributed, it has never been easier for your competitors to reach your customers, and for your customers to buy from your competitors. It is now more critical than ever, therefore, to focus your Engine B on your end customer. If you're selling B2B, then it's important to focus not only on your customer but also on your customer's customer (B2B2C). This may sound obvious, but we've seen plenty of organisations obsess over their bottom line instead of putting the customer first and building strong, lasting relationships that drive long-term success.

So what does this mean for your Engine B's structure? Well, rather than focusing on a single item in isolation, you need to focus on the journeys your customers take as they interact with you. Your teams need to work through and design each touchpoint, as well as what happens in between. The goal is to effectively storyboard the ideal customer lifecycle, both online and offline. Your Engine B isn't about improving what you currently do; rather, it's about meeting the needs of customers — whether current ones or potential customers in untapped markets — in the best possible way, and in doing so, unlocking new forms of revenue. Because your Engine B will be built with minimal legacy, you are free to design directly for the customer, from scratch. Therefore you need to view technology not as a constraint, but rather as an enabler. Be bold, and ask the question, if I could do anything to meet the needs of my customer, what would that entail? When answering this question, don't just look within your current market for guidance; look to the organisations and sectors that are synonymous with innovation and customer centrism. But, again, don't just look at the obvious, such as the tech giants like Amazon and Google; dig deeper, and look to smaller companies thriving in emerging markets. More than just inspiration, you may find new market opportunities or even possible partnerships.

Once you have the ideal customer experience mapped out, design the infrastructure to support it. In the digital age this means a combination of technological, human and physical resources. Traditionally, online and offline were treated as quite distinct areas, meaning digital channels were built as standalone items. This perspective is obsolete, and in fact detrimental to your organisation. Digital technologies and physical infrastructure need to be viewed together, as keeping them separated leads to extremely disjointed experiences, which in the digital age is fatal. Human resources are vital to ensure the organisation stays creative and to maintain important relationships. Therefore, when designing the infrastructure to support the ideal customer experience you have developed, scrap the outdated view of maintaining distinct technology and business teams, and instead focus on creating customer-centric teams designed to provide the best possible experience. Design everything for the customer.

Questions

1. How many of the processes and structures in your current business would you have in place if you were starting again?

2. How much are you investing in systems and processes that are likely to be replaced by Engine B?

3. Without Engine B and a new strategy, how long will your business survive in our new economy?

4. Fill in the blank: _____ is the single common goal across our business that is shared by both Engine A and B.

5. Are you clear on the focus needed in Engine A?

6. What different metrics will you use for Engine B?

7. Is your core growth engine missing opportunities? If so, what are the barriers blocking you and are they necessary or antiquated bureaucracy?

8. What does the customer want, and if you were starting a company from scratch, how would you deliver it to them?

9. Fill in the blank: In _____ months we expect Engine B to take over from Engine A in economic terms.

Chapter summary

Your business needs a new design and a better way to execute it. Implementing the strategies for success described in chapter 1 is critical. At the same time, you need to sustain the success and cash generation potential of your current business. Two power plants, Engines A and B, are better than one if you want your business to stay in the air.

Managing the demand for resources of both teams, and keeping everyone focused on a single common goal, is a challenge. Engine A is getting ready for decommissioning, so the speed and focus of Engine B is critically important. Figure 2.1 summarises the key attributes of, and relationship between, Engines A and B.

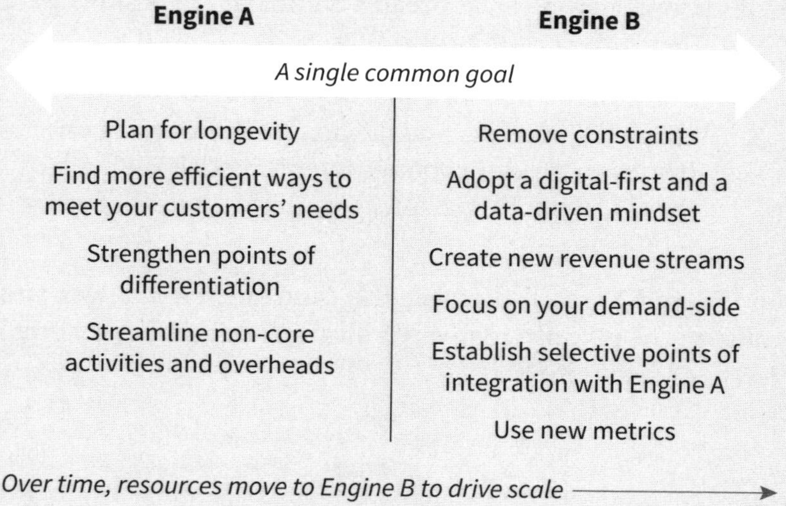

Engine A	Engine B
A single common goal	
Plan for longevity	Remove constraints
Find more efficient ways to meet your customers' needs	Adopt a digital-first and a data-driven mindset
Strengthen points of differentiation	Create new revenue streams
Streamline non-core activities and overheads	Focus on your demand-side
	Establish selective points of integration with Engine A
	Use new metrics

Over time, resources move to Engine B to drive scale ⟶

Figure 2.1: Engines A and B

There are four key areas you need to focus on with regard to Engine B:

1. **Support and empower your Engine B team.** While your Engine B team should have complete autonomy, it should also leverage the capabilities, IP and resources of your core business. Remember, your objective is that Engine B will eventually become your primary economic engine, so make sure you give it the right fuel to get out of first gear.

2. **Software will be at the heart of your value and delivery model.** Software allows your business to scale exponentially and allows people to focus on high-value activities, such as customer relationships.

3. **A data-driven leadership mindset is key.** Data's ability to help drive operational performance and create new revenue streams is critical. Think about data first and everything else afterwards.

4. **Start on the demand side of your business.** In chapter 1, we explained the reasons for focusing on the demand side of your economic model. We covered these again in this chapter within the context of your Engine B.

In chapter 3, you'll discover the fundamental changes you must make to your company culture to tackle the external forces of disruption.

CHAPTER 3
Culture

*Whosoever desires constant success must
change his conduct with the times.*
Niccolò Machiavelli

As organisations grow, teams and business units begin to segregate. So entrenched is this pattern that anthropologist Robin Dunbar developed a theory about it. He proposed that the number of meaningful relationships a single person can have is limited to 150. In the workplace, this extends to a natural threshold of the number of people able to work together productively. When it comes to running an organisation with thousands of employees, it's no wonder that 'silos' form and trusted relationships falter when groups start to compete against each other rather than collaborate. Some organisations defy this trend, however, unifying their employees despite their differences, structure and scale. Think about companies like Johnson & Johnson, The Walt Disney Company, Amazon and Google. How do they create cohesion and foster productivity? And more importantly, what aspects of great corporate culture do you need to focus on as you build a digitally enabled business?

Company culture is created in exactly the same fashion as a religion or democracy. Behaviours created from the organisation's inception are reinforced over time by leadership, attracting like-minded people and eventually reaching critical mass to become an accepted 'truth'. These truths drive performance, priorities, and the countless everyday decisions an employee makes without guidance or oversight. A recent survey conducted by Capgemini found that 62 per cent of respondents viewed culture as the number one hurdle to achieving an effective digital transformation. The pivot points required in chapter 1, and the rethinking of structures in chapter 2, will succeed or fail based on the nature and strength of your company culture. In this chapter, we'll help you determine whether your current culture will help or hinder your digital transformation. You'll also discover five cornerstones of a digital culture, and six ways to build a digitally mature team.

Will your culture help or hinder?

Achieving your preferred culture is easier if you know and understand your starting position and spend the time needed to identify what needs to change to support your transformation. One widely used model that helps establish this is the Competing Values Framework (see figure 3.1). Developed by Kim Cameron and Robert Quinn in the 1980s, and based on empirical research from more than 1000 organisations, it identifies two major dimensions of organisational effectiveness:

» the extent to which the organisation has an internal focus and integration versus external focus and differentiation

» its preference for stability and control versus flexibility and discretion.

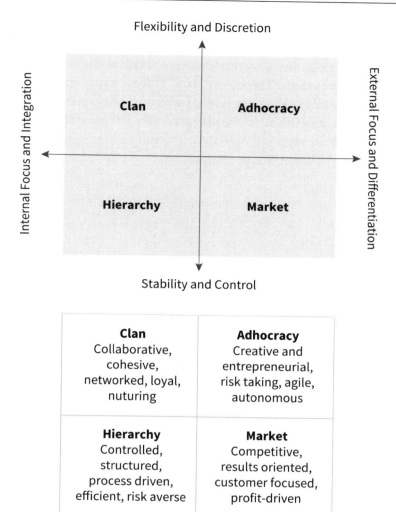

Figure 3.1: Cameron and Quinn's Competing Values Framework

These dimensions represent competing values for the organisation and form the axes that separate four distinct culture-type quadrants, each with its own set of characteristics. Once assessed, it is natural that over time your organisation develops a leading cultural type, and usually a mix of the four quadrants, in its profile. The balance of profiles can change over time as the organisation matures or is exposed to different external pressures. There is no 'bad' culture type, and there is a place for all types of employees across the organisation. The key is to ensure the overall cultural profile of the organisation is able to deliver outcomes needed in its competitive environment and respond when things change.

This framework is often used to map the gap between the current state and the preferred future state for the organisation, in preparation for a significant change or transformation.

Cameron and Quinn conclude that a successful organisation is a flexible one, able to draw on all four culture types from among its ranks as the competitive environment requires. Even a cursory understanding of their model raises awareness of the quantum of cultural change that may be needed to support your organisation's shift from where it is today to embrace a more digital mindset. As we discuss later in this chapter, transitioning to a digital culture generally requires more emphasis on behaviours and values associated with the adhocracy and clan culture types. This is driven by the speed of the market, the need for self-organisation and autonomy to enable teams to innovate, develop and launch in shorter cycles, and the relentless need to focus on the customer.

At the other extreme, hierarchy cultures that are predominantly focused on stability and control — protecting revenue, highly process driven, with a heavy reliance on senior decision making — will impede transformation efforts unless you intervene. According to Cameron and Quinn, hierarchies are the most difficult cultures to change, as their natural inertia means it's 'almost as if gravity takes over', ossifying structure and process as the organisation matures, pushing it down the matrix towards less flexible, and more internally focused behaviour.

The cornerstones of a digital culture

We believe there are five principles that are critical to establishing a digital culture, and they are intrinsically linked to the other structural issues you need to consider as you transform your business.

FREE FLOW OF INFORMATION

Information and data must be able to move seamlessly throughout the organisation, as well as between your company and your customers. It is imperative that data, new findings and best practice are shared easily so teams can work together to find the best solutions. Information must also flow freely between your business units and customers to ensure your company is customer driven. In chapter 4, we go into greater detail on how to improve the flow of data throughout your organisation.

CUSTOMER FOCUS

If you don't know what your customer wants, then you may as well pack up now. Understand the difference between their needs and their wants, then execute on their needs — even if they don't know what these are yet. As Henry Ford said, 'If I had asked my customers what they wanted, they would have said a faster horse.' For detail on understanding customer needs, refer back to chapter 2 and the section on building Engine A. If you can deliver what customers want while providing them with a fantastic experience, then they'll always come back. Just don't forget that the customer's expectations never stay the same over time.

AGILITY

With the digital economy moving faster than ever before, your teams have to be able to react to this change. First-mover advantage is critical in the information age to stealing a march on the competition, while moving faster than anyone else ensures you stay in front. Long-winded decision-making processes must be streamlined, and employees must be flexible in the face of change. Your Engine B team, profiled in chapter 2, should champion this new pace and style.

INQUISITIVENESS

Create a culture that is always on the lookout for new opportunities and where failure isn't considered taboo. Remember, you can only really learn by failing. Companies that are willing to take calculated risks on novel ideas, even though they may require self-disruption, are the ones that thrive in the digital economy. Chapter 7 shows you how to incorporate innovation into your long-term strategy for investment and growth.

EMPLOYEE EXPERIENCE AND ENGAGEMENT

A thriving digital culture must provide teams with an environment in which they are challenged, learn new things and have the freedom to make decisions on their own. A highly engaged team is the most productive, and with recent studies showing that only 33 per cent of the workforce is engaged, getting this right creates competitive advantage. Key to an engaged workforce is the personal connection employees make with their organisation and the sense that their work and individual strengths are valued. This can be achieved through focus on activating purpose, or the 'why' of the work as part of your company vision, ensuring clear performance expectations; regular coaching and recognition; and giving employees the tools, environment and autonomy to excel.

Building a digitally mature team

A digital culture is underpinned by a high level of digital maturity. This may seem obvious, but without this maturity, everything remains static. Putting up motivational posters and throwing around buzzwords may give the impression that the company is transforming itself, but in reality, these types of initiatives don't alter the company's underlying foundations. Rather, they create confusion and scepticism about the value of, and rationale for, the change that is so desperately needed. Digital maturity is both a mindset and a skillset. Save your campaign for when you have in place a program of systematic leadership, behavioural and process change, and some achievements to acknowledge.

Digitally mature teams understand that what they must do now is different from what they did in the past, which is also different from what they will have to do in the future. Here, we identify six key steps to building a digitally mature team.

START WITH VISIBLE LEADERSHIP

Without a mature digital culture that is defined, championed and modelled from the top down, your organisation will be unable to navigate the relentless waves of change and the gravitational pull of your company's legacy approach to managing pre-digital disruption, particularly if your predominant company culture type is less flexible and process driven. Digital maturity is not the responsibility of a few individuals in functional roles; it must be led by the CEO and executive team. It requires an acceptance that the traditional roles played by leaders need to change and that new talent may also be required. This is confronting stuff for many who have worked their way to the top through years of pre-digital achievement. Survey findings from Capgemini support this, suggesting that the inability of leadership to acknowledge the degree of culture change needed is a key contributor to failed transformation efforts. Left unaddressed, it can drive a damaging disconnect between leadership and employees, and their perceptions of progress towards a digital culture and behaviours in the organisation.

Defining and communicating the values that underpin your digital culture is critical if you are to build employee engagement and alignment. Leadership must be its most passionate advocate. However, the change also needs to translate into tangible business outcomes, achieved through changes in process, KPIs and recognition systems that reward the right behaviours. For example, there is little point introducing a cultural change focused on collaboration if performance measures contradict and/or discourage teams from working together.

Company culture codes have frequently been developed in the start-up and technology community to identify and drive desired values and behaviours from the earliest establishment phase of a new venture. Recognising that culture will develop regardless, these codes are a transparent and conscious way to establish the expected way of working, similar to the principles applied in determining the preferred future state as part of the Competing Values Framework cultural assessment. These codes are written using simple, dynamic plain speak. Take one of HubSpot's, for example: 'We commit maniacally to both our mission and metrics'. Or Netflix: 'Context not Control' and 'Highly Aligned, Loosely Coupled'. Culture codes take a company mission or values statement a step further by broadly describing what they mean for employee behaviour, decision making, prioritisation of focus and employee success. What's more, as these codes have been developed within digital organisations, they hint at ways of working that you can leverage as part of your own transformation efforts. Luckily, given they support talent attraction, big-tech culture codes tend to be freely shared and published.

Compare the codes of digital organisations with your own mission statements and articulation of company values, and dedicate time as an executive team to make the changes necessary to realign with your digital vision. This requires some soul searching and discussion. An early published version of Netflix's culture code reflected that Enron's values were Integrity, Communication, Respect and Excellence, which, although admirable, were completely at odds with the people and behaviours that were rewarded. Plain speak codes help cut through platitude. However, it is how you as a leadership team live it, reinforce it with the decisions you make, and reward those who best represent who you want to be as a digital organisation, that will drive the greatest sustainable change.

BUST THE SILOS

Mini-empires are a huge killer of cultural change efforts. Empires create borders, which create silos, hindering how information travels between teams, leading to varied goals and ambitions. It's imperative that these borders are broken down and that collaboration between teams becomes the new norm. In short, best practice and capability needs to be shared by all.

One way to bust the silos is to identify the core customer-driven activities that support your value chain. As a simple example, think of customer service support in a company that makes and sells a physical product. The sales team, contact centre, accounts team, and marketing and delivery team all interact with the customer. Some of these steps may even be managed by third parties. Perhaps there is a customer relationship management (CRM) system that keeps track of interactions. Now think about how and where those activities are currently delivered across your organisation. Are all of the people involved in providing service support connected horizontally to ensure communication, knowledge and the best possible service across the value chain? Often employees are not even aware of others outside of their function or responsibility area, what they know or the constraints they have. This can lead to duplication and inconsistency for the customer. Join these people up. Unite them around the customer need, and promote the flow of information between them through shared physical workspaces, virtual collaboration spaces or common goals. This weakens the functional silo, and strengthens the commitment to the broader team and the end-to-end customer outcome. Cross-functional teaming will improve agility, sharing of ideas and removal of bottlenecks. Most importantly, it will build trust across the business, enabling it to grow faster.

EDUCATE

Sometimes resistance to change comes simply from a lack of understanding. When you talk about what digital means, people may nod and smile, but that doesn't mean they truly understand it. Those who aren't born digital can learn. As a matter of fact, individuals who immerse themselves in the topic, and turn this foreign concept into their domain, can play a significant role in your company's digital transformation. Not only do they truly understand the ins and outs of your organisation, but they also understand the implications of digital on the business. And, most importantly, they are capable of surviving change, which makes a truly powerful trifecta that will help steer any organisation through the fog of change.

Therefore, key to driving a digital mindset in any workforce is education, upskilling and action. Encourage a mindset that looks outward. The acquisition of knowledge is no longer restricted to those who can afford it; learning opportunities are everywhere and do not need to be developed in-house. A program combining mobile learning, forums for discussion, speaking events, and encouragement to experiment and apply digital principles to everyday work will go a long way to helping your people along the curve. When it comes to upskilling, add digital competencies to your skills framework and assess your organisation's maturity. Be prepared to acknowledge that leadership and senior management may have the greatest gap to close. Remember that curiosity and a desire to learn are the most important attributes you can foster in an environment where change is a constant.

Thinking back to the Competing Values Framework, if you are transitioning your organisation from a culture that has been more internally focused, reorienting your teams back to their customers may be more important in the short to medium term than meeting the requirements of the internal machine. Building customer relationships is not just the responsibility of the sales team. A customer experience (CX) strategy across the company highlights the touchpoints and 'moments of truth' your customers have with you across your entire business (known as journeys), designed around principles that drive an optimal experience. If you want your teams to transition from process focused to customer focused, developing a CX strategy helps put everything in perspective, and enables you to focus investment and priorities around your customers. Once established, regular feedback loops are important to ensure your teams are working directly with the customer. In many cases, this can mean creating new roles within your business focused on providing more value to them faster, as well as implementing channels for your customers and teams to interact and communicate with one another.

DECENTRALISE DECISION MAKING

Is decision making in your organisation bound by a hierarchy culture and its by-product, the meeting mania of senior leaders? Delaying a decision because you can't access the decision makers kills agility in your organisation and confirms that you favour process over customer. Key to creating a successful digital culture is decentralising decision making, ensuring that those who are close to your customers and data are able to make decisions autonomously, rather than going through rigorous decision-making processes. Empowering and trusting people to make the right decisions frees your company to move quickly and not lag in the face of change. Over time, this empowerment will perpetuate itself as teams take ownership over their projects and outputs, pushing themselves to provide more value to your customers.

As a leader, you can find it hard to let go, but now you need to rethink your whole decision-making process. Rather than encouraging big decisions that cannot be changed, incentivise your teams to make smaller decisions at a faster pace. It's also important to minimise the number of decisions that cannot be revoked, which is exactly what digital technology enables you to do through making small investments that can have a big impact. Agreeing on the non-negotiables, such as underlying infrastructure, signifies that everything else is flexible within parameters. Smaller decisions mean less time is required to gather information, which also complements the fast-paced nature of the digital economy. If you have positioned your teams closer to the customer, and provided them with the channels to communicate effectively and collect meaningful data, they should have more than enough information to make smart decisions.

ENCOURAGE TEAM DIVERSITY AND CANDOUR

Changing your culture should go hand in hand with changing how your teams operate. A digital team needs to be stubborn in their commitment to execute, but also open and flexible to pivot at the drop of a hat. This may seem like a paradox, but what it really means is having a concrete vision that everyone believes in, then being fluid in terms of how you achieve this vision.

Diversity within teams encourages new and novel solutions to hard problems. As a leader, you need to be focused on diversity of thinking. Diversity of thinking enables organisations to identify new ways of doing things through varied perspectives working together. It goes well beyond race, gender or age to focus on people's innate individual characteristics and abilities, creating an organisation that is powered by openness, collaboration and acceptance. Make sure diversity of thought is both applauded and protected. As Kim Scott, author of *Radical Candor*, puts it, 'The fastest path to artificial relationships at work, and to the gravitational pull of organizational mediocrity, is to insist that everyone have the same worldview before building relationships with them.' Do not allow the status quo to dilute or, worse, intimidate and quash fresh perspectives.

To encourage diversity of thinking, identify skill gaps and style gaps, and hire people to fill them. Actively look to hire people who will cause some friction and prompt debate. Through bringing different strengths and ideas to the table, employees will be able to engage and work with one another, while also challenging themselves and their peers, developing new and innovative solutions as your company digitally transforms itself. This can take some time to develop. However, as teams learn to embrace a feedback culture and manage differences respectfully, they also develop high levels of trust. In this way diversity of thinking creates teams that not only embrace change but thrive on it.

FOCUS ON DELIVERY

Digital delivery is a whole new kettle of fish. Cloud enables an extremely cost-effective and quick way to market. This has created a whole new level of software delivery through leveraging the cloud, platforms and data. Monolithic IT projects that traditionally could have taken years can now be broken down and delivered in weeks, at a fraction of the cost. Being able to deliver smaller chunks of value cost-effectively is an incredibly powerful thing. For one thing, ascertaining buy-in from other leaders within the organisation becomes a much easier task, because you are effectively offering them bite-sized chunks of value for small amounts of money, which traditionally was just not possible. That alone is positive, but there are a couple of other benefits associated with this kind of delivery model.

1. Decrease the risk and increase the appetite

At the very beginning of a project, the associated risk is at its highest. Once the project is complete, the risk decreases to zero. Longer projects inherently bring with them more risk as there is more opportunity for things to change and to go wrong. Being able to bring ideas to market quicker, as well as being able to divide larger projects into phases that still provide value, significantly decreases the risk. This means that business cases become much more palatable and projects much more likely to fall within budget, which used to be unheard of in the land of IT delivery.

Now executives no longer have to worry about spending millions of dollars on new software products. As the appetite for digital increases, teams can look to trial more 'out there' technologies and ideas that no manager would previously have signed off on, as the risk and price were too high. Key stakeholders within your executive team will suddenly be very interested in piloting new and novel technology, pushing teams and your organisation as a whole to be more creative and innovative.

2. Increase the wins and losses

Shorter project timeframes mean more opportunity for wins. Wins are a massive confidence booster for teams. This creates a delivery flywheel, where teams receive positive feedback from both customer and management through increasing the value they provide, and they are naturally motivated to repeat the success, generating more positive feedback. It's important that these feedback channels are strong and healthy. Success begets success, and as your teams continue to deliver, momentum will build and your organisation will transform into a digital delivery machine.

As with any culture that encourages experimentation, there will be losses. That's fine. In fact, it's beneficial. Failures are the most important source of learning in an organisation. What's great about delivering in the digital age is that costs are extremely low, and projects smaller and more iterative, so decisions can be easily reverted or rolled back. After any unsuccessful project, run a retrospective to determine the root cause of the failure, then share this finding with your organisation. Treat all missteps as valuable lessons that in the long run will help fuel the wins.

Questions

1. Have you assessed your company culture and the quantum of change needed to support your digital transformation?

2. Have you clearly articulated what underpins your digital culture, and does it resonate with your customers and employees?

3. How aligned is your performance and reward system to your preferred culture and behaviours?

4. Do you have sufficient cognitive diversity in your leadership team to address new and unexpected strategic problems successfully?

5. Can your teams move fast enough, and do they have the necessary skills, decision rights and information to meet the needs of the changing buyer?

6. How can you move your employees closer to the customer?

7. Are your employees empowered to take calculated risks, and are they encouraged to learn from failures, rather than be penalised for them?

Chapter summary

Do not overlook the importance of culture in driving your digital transformation. It is highly likely that it is time to refresh the company myths that have underpinned your success to date, and incorporate new cultural 'truths' into your employees' everyday work and behaviours. To do this, you need to undertake a frank assessment of where you are today either through guided discussion or by utilising a diagnostic assessment (the Competing Values Framework illustrated is one approach) to determine the gap between your current and preferred future state, and the quantum of change needed. Agree with your leadership peers to rebalance your organisation as required to adopt the cultural attributes proven to support success in a digital world.

None of this change is possible without the mindset of curiosity to keep testing and pursuing new ideas and improvements (accepting that some of these will fail), and nowhere is this attitude more important than in the leadership team. With strong leadership, resistance to change can be broken down, and changes in hierarchy and decision making can be made, allowing teams to focus on performance and delivery, rather than worrying about getting sign-off from management. Embrace flexibility. In a nutshell, this means getting closer to your customers and incorporating their feedback, promoting the free flow of information, and increasing agility through greater autonomy and self-organisation. Ultimately, changing your delivery model will accrue the greatest benefits for your organisation, and continually reinforce and perpetuate the culture that will drive success for you in the future.

This brings us to the end of part I. In part II you'll discover the three digital enablers that will transform your company.

Part II
Digital enablers for transformation

The big decisions — strategy, organisational design and culture — are the bedrock of your digital transformation. Getting these big decisions right will be vital in part II, where we unpack the core digital capabilities you need to focus on in your digital transformation to ensure you stay competitive in the new economy.

At a conceptual level, we define digital as a data-oriented mindset — a belief that the applications, insights and business opportunities from data are limitless and, because of this, will redefine entire markets. At a practical level, digital is about the application of certain kinds of technology, by which we mean designing, building and operating those technologies in a particular way.

When it comes to investing in technology, pre-digital incumbents often don't know what technology or technologies to prioritise. Leaders are besieged by journalists, thought leaders and marketing teams who preach and promise about the future of tech. Further, technology changes so fast that what's considered cutting-edge today is obsolete tomorrow. When prioritising, we encourage you to focus on structure and purpose, rather than specific technologies. It's important to get the backbone right. Once you do, the rest will fall into place.

We call this backbone the digital enablement. This is not technology per se, but rather a core set of capabilities that will bolster your business's digital maturity. If you think of strategy, organisational design and culture as the foundations of your castle and moat, then the digital enablers are your buttresses and columns. Structurally, the two must be aligned to successfully support your digital transformation.

Through analysing many companies and business models, we've found there are just three digital enablers that, as a pre-digital incumbent, you need to focus on: data, platforms and systems of intelligence (business-driven artificial intelligence). These three enablers have been fundamental to the success of some of the biggest tech companies over the past 10 years, such as Google, Amazon and Facebook. They also have the potential to transform your organisation from a static — dare we say, medieval — fortress susceptible to attack, into a highly competitive and productive machine. Our experience indicates that the application of these enablers (above anything else) is central to the architecture of digital success.

So why data, platforms and systems of intelligence? Fundamentally, each on their own brings to the organisation incredible opportunities, whether it be the insights you garner from your data, the customers and third parties you connect with on your platform, or the internal efficiencies and enhanced customer experiences you derive from your systems of intelligence. But together, with these three enablers working in harmony, this is where the magic happens. If you cast your mind back to the flywheel we discussed in chapter 1, you'll start to get a better understanding of how these three enablers fit into the design of a digital business.

Figure A represents the phases of building the flywheel. If we group components, you'll understand how the three enablers complement one another. Box 1 represents the platform that facilitates interactions and exchanges between you, your customers and third parties. Box 2 represents the data you collect from these interactions. Finally, Box 3 depicts where you apply systems of intelligence, fuelled by this data, which is collected from your customers, employees and processes, continuously improving the experience you provide, as well as your internal efficiencies. As you can see, each of the enablers sustains the others, so implementing all three is critical to the success of your flywheel.

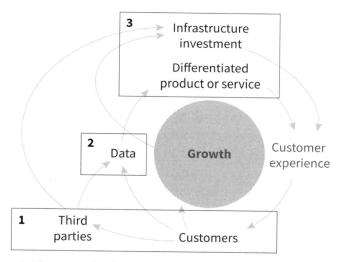

Figure A: the growth of the flywheel

Source: Adapted from the Virtuous Cycle, as drawn by Amazon and adapted by Sam Seely.

The big tech companies, which we would classify as digitally mature, have mastered the flywheel and the three digital enablers. Now it's your turn. To begin this journey, you need to measure your baseline digital maturity to help you understand where to focus your attention first.

The application of data, platforms and systems of intelligence can be structured as a formula that describes your organisation's overall digital maturity from a technology standpoint. We certainly don't want to downplay the importance of your strategy, organisational design and culture, but without effectively implementing the three digital enablers, you ultimately cannot compete.

Imagine your organisation's digital maturity is represented as an overall index — a score out of, say, 10 or 100. The function itself is derived from the individual maturity score you assess for each of data, platforms and systems of intelligence. The formula looks like this:

Digital Maturity Index = ∫ (Data, Platforms, Systems of Intelligence)

In the next three chapters, we will explain in detail how to think about each of the three digital enablers and how to apply these to your business, linking each one back to the big decisions you've made about strategies for success, organisational design and culture. After reading all three chapters, return to this formula to assess your digital maturity. This will help you to identify your strengths and weaknesses, which will guide your digital roadmap.

CHAPTER 4
Data

*It is a capital mistake to theorize
before one has data.*
Sherlock Holmes

Data is often referred to as the new oil, and for good reason. It is the critical fuel for your business's new economic engine and your digital strategy.

Most pre-digital incumbents have a data value problem. That is, they struggle to gain business value from all the data, or any of the data, they are collecting. This mass of data has become known as *big data*, with many companies investing heavily in the infrastructure and skills required to support it. According to Dresner Advisory Services' 2017 Big Data Analytics Market Study, 53 per cent of global companies reported that they 'use big data today', compared with 17 per cent in 2015. Notably, there is still regional variation in the use of big data: North America (55 per cent) narrowly leads the Europe, Middle East and Africa region (53 per cent) in its current levels of big-data analytics adoption. Asia–Pacific respondents report 44 per cent current adoption and are most likely to say they 'may use big data in the future'. However, according to a 2016 survey by technology research company Gartner, of the companies that had invested in big-data capabilities, only 15 per cent reported a live big-data project. This reflects the lack of capability required to drive value from data. Known as the *data value gap* (see figure 4.1), this is either your biggest threat or your greatest opportunity.

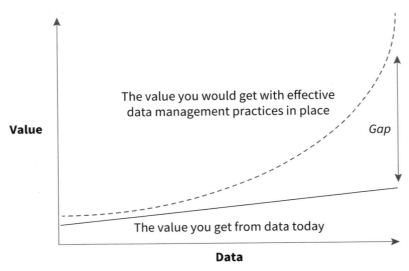

Figure 4.1: the data value gap

This chapter will help you focus on data value and opening up opportunities to drive business growth. You'll discover three key things you need to know about data, and what you can learn from car manufacturer Tesla. We'll also discuss the application of *thick data*, present a five-step framework to harness and apply data, and reveal three key areas where data can drive growth.

Three things you need to know about data

The rise of big data, and the associated realisation of its importance, has been accompanied by a major misconception: the idea that data volume alone is the most important consideration. Having more data is great, but it isn't everything. The value and application of data to your business strategy is what really counts. There are three factors you need to consider when thinking about data within your business.

GRANULARITY

The granularity of your data is instrumental in helping make insights not just directional but specific. Granular data helps you bridge the gap between your strategy and your execution. For example, when you know your customers' buying habits and preferences in detail, you can focus on specific customers in specific circumstances within your marketing campaign. Data granularity directly impacts the accuracy of each prediction and your return on investment.

SOURCE AND THE CONNECTIONS WITHIN

Having customer, transactional, supplier or usage data sitting in silos makes it difficult to use. Connections between related types of data help you answer questions like: which customer will buy if I run a promotional offer on this product? To do this, you need to know your customers' shopping history, as well as their profile and preferences, and the correlation in style between the product you want to sell and the products you've already sold. The answer may be hard to conceptualise and difficult to intuit, which is where *data science* and *data modelling* come into play. Both data science and data modelling are terms used to describe the connections between data and the process of gaining insights from it. That said, if you are going to build these models, your data needs to be centralised and accessible, which for many pre-digital incumbents is not the case. This process will be explained further in this chapter.

QUALITY AND COMPLETENESS

There's a saying, 'Garbage in, garbage out', that captures it. If the data you use is incomplete or inaccurate, the resulting predictions will be useless. There are a number of techniques for machines to help improve data quality or statistical methods and mitigate the effect of outliers. As a general rule, however, you should focus on more than just data quantity — quality is also very important.

High-quality data is data that meets the needs of the analysis required, and accurately represents real-world information or constructs. Low-quality data can have a significant impact on a company's strategy, resulting in higher operating costs, lower customer satisfaction, poorer decision making and diminished internal trust around decisions.

Over the course of the rest of the chapter we will explain how these factors influence the way in which you approach data and the strategy you employ.

Data on wheels

What happens when a company builds its entire business model around data? Well, if you take a look at Tesla, one of multi-billionaire Elon Musk's most reputable companies and a considerable data aggregator, you'll see that data has played an integral role in defining the company's success.

Tesla, which, as of April 2017, is the United States' most valuable car manufacturer, heavily employs a data-driven mindset. Since the introduction of the electric Model S in 2012, Tesla has in fact become one of the most valuable companies in the world, and has forced a rethink of strategy for Volkswagen, Renault-Nissan, Hyundai-Kia and General Motors, the automotive industry's traditional powerhouses over the past few decades.

When you think of car manufacturers, you most likely think of mechanical and automotive engineers. Tesla is a far cry from that, with a huge team of software developers and testers who work across a range of projects, including the development of in-vehicle systems, driverless technology and solar panels.

Tesla cars self-report data that is recorded and transmitted to central servers. This data has a number of uses. If, for example, vehicles are detecting faulty pumps, this information can be processed and a model built that can predict a specific pump failure before it occurs. The car will then notify the driver, who will be prompted to visit a Tesla mechanic before any problem arises. If an issue is critical, Tesla will save time by sending a mechanic to the owner's home. In the future, driverless cars will automatically drive themselves to repair shops for diagnostics and troubleshooting while not in use.

A Tesla vehicle is a data magnet. The company's ability to redeploy data through operations to create a better, safer driver experience is an extremely powerful competitive advantage. No other car manufacturer has such a data- and software-driven system in place.

Data not only improves the driver experience, but allows Tesla to continuously optimise its supply chain by identifying opportunities to improve its vehicles, which could involve replacing a particular supplier, using a different model of a certain part or even re-engineering. Further, the data is useful not only in identifying what to do, but also for understanding the underlying reasons for failures. In some cases, it may be due to poor-quality materials, while in others it may be a human error or a shortcoming in the process itself. This is essential, because if you understand the root cause of failure, it's much easier to find a solution to the issue.

The key lesson from Tesla is that a data-driven mindset has not just changed the product, but has begun to reshape an entire industry. Studying this new business model, you will get the sense that everything Tesla does is fact-based and designed to optimise an overarching set of objectives — sales, product quality, maintenance costs and supply chain efficiency. Uncovering and satisfying customer needs becomes more than an imperative — it is the norm. With a data-driven approach there is also nowhere to hide, so decisions are made with greater levels of transparency.

The application of thick data

In 2015, the big-data industry was worth $122 billion. The International Data Corporation expects this to grow to more than $187 billion in 2019, an increase of more than 50 per cent over the five-year forecast period. These figures clearly demonstrate that businesses are spending big on big data. And yet, according to ethnographer and big-data expert Tricia Wang, 73 per cent of big-data initiatives in 2015 were not profitable.

Examples of where big data is applied range from optimising delivery logistics to helping manage genetic coding issues. Not all systems can be neatly contained, however, and when you are dealing with variables that change, especially when humans are involved, outcomes can be unpredictable. Take the stock market, for example. For decades, people have searched for patterns in the stock market that could lead to riches, but the key has proved elusive both because the system itself continues to change and because humans, who are highly erratic and unpredictable, are involved. There is an important distinction between quantitative and contained systems versus dynamic systems. Quantitative and contained systems do not change, and typically they do not involve humans. A dynamic system, on the other hand, does change and is influenced by human behaviour — an infinitive variable. The whole, evolving field of behavioural economics exists to explain and predict human irrationality; for our purposes here, it is enough to flag that people — your customers — introduce a mercurial element to any data model. As astrophysicist Neil deGrasse Tyson said in 2016, 'In science, when human behaviour enters the equation, things go nonlinear. That's why physics is easy and sociology is hard.'

When humans and big data clash, a paradox emerges. Big data answers questions that humans would otherwise find hard to resolve. However, predictions from big data raise more questions when humans are involved. In addition, a bias can occur where humans unconsciously value the measurable over the immeasurable. The healthcare industry offers a good example of this. Patient wellbeing, especially when psychological in nature, can be difficult to assess. Nonetheless reviews of hospitals and care providers are conducted, and practitioners are punished or rewarded on quantified performance.

When dealing with data, it's important to recognise that not everything that's valuable is directly measurable. To ensure valuable insights don't slip through the gaps, your big-data systems need people who can gather *thick data* — that is, precious information from humans, stories, emotions and interactions that cannot be quantified. Consider enlisting the help of an ethnographer — someone who can take a scientific approach to observing a culture or group — to help find this information. Thick data can come in small sizes, such as a brief statement from a user about their experience with a new device, but it can also be deeply insightful, covering many perspectives related to the experience. Most importantly, this qualitative material helps provide the context around your big-data models. Big data is able to provide insights at scale through standardising and normalising aggregated data, whereas thick data can help rescue the context and 'human' element that is lost from making big data usable. When you integrate the two, you get to ask the million-dollar question: Why?

For example, Netflix was able to leverage both big data and thick data to provide a better experience to its user base. Netflix was more successful when it hired a thick-data expert — someone who knows how to ask questions of customers related to what they need and to test what they want. In doing so, Netflix discovered its customers love to binge-watch TV and they don't feel guilty doing it. This led Netflix to redesign the viewer experience to encourage binge-watching by releasing the entire first series of *House of Cards* in 2013. By leveraging this thick-data insight, Netflix not only improved its business, but also changed the way its customers watch and consume content.

A framework to harness and apply data

Data should not merely support your business — it should play a strategic role and provide value as a driver of growth. We've identified five steps to achieving this outcome, known as the Data Value Framework (see figure 4.2).

1. START WITH STRATEGY

In part I of this book, we discussed the strategies for success in our new economy, the organisational design you need to execute and the culture required to sustain your approach. Now think again about strategies for success. What insights from data will help differentiate your product or service or provide you with a competitive advantage? Consider the data you need to make money and drive your economic engine today, then the data you want given an alternative value chain. Thinking like this will help you prioritise the data you need.

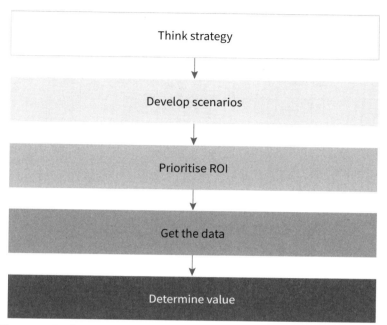

Figure 4.2: the Data Value Framework

2. IDENTIFY AND VALIDATE SUPPORTING SCENARIOS

Step 2 involves taking the ideas captured in step 1 and grouping them into specific actions, or *use cases*, your organisation can realistically undertake. For each of these scenarios, you should identify not only the sources of business value, but also the implementation challenges that are obvious at this stage. Map out each use case using a consistent template; the widely circulated 'business model canvas' (see figure 4.3, overleaf) is one type of quick synopsis that can help you compare the relative strengths, weaknesses and potential impact of each scenario to address your strategic priorities.

Throughout this exercise, you need to consider factors such as risk, privacy, levels of access, availability of data, ease of accessing accurate information, and how it should be organised for your end purposes. To move forward from this point, you need to be keenly aware of what it is you want to do, and what you need to know to do it.

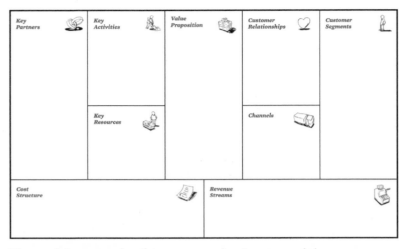

Figure 4.3: example of a one-page business model canvas

Source: © Osterwalder, A. 2009. *Business Model Generation: A Handbook for Visionaries, Game Changers, and Challengers.* John Wiley and Sons Inc.

3. PRIORITISE BASED ON RETURN ON INVESTMENT

You may find this step the most difficult because it requires you to do two things that many large companies struggle to do: prioritise and focus. Prioritising and focusing are not popular concepts for many organisations because of political and organisational pressures. As discussed in chapter 2, consensus is hard to achieve when there are many agendas. Articulating alternative scenarios in step 2 will help you lay out a logical progression of steps to build your big-data capabilities through a series of initiatives through which data and analytics are increasingly woven into the fabric of your business operations. Trying to do it all at once will only end in wasted resources and lacklustre results.

If you can convince your organisation to build out a big-data business strategy one use case at a time, it will enable you to become an expert at harvesting data, building analytics tools relevant to your organisation and applying those tools to subsequent use cases. Seek opportunities to demonstrate ROI in each step of the process, both to manage your stakeholders and as a way to gauge the impact of your initiatives.

4. GET THE DATA

In step 4, you need to work with your team to brainstorm different data sources that can support your top-priority use cases. Step 2's focus on implementation and potential challenges should have laid the groundwork for these conversations. In most cases, data gathering will be an iterative process, because data science naturally focuses on the variables that better predict business or operational performance. Your team will learn as it goes what data proves most valuable for your end purposes. Ensure business stakeholders can collaborate with the data science team to identify and test different data sources that might yield the best predictive models.

5. DETERMINE THE ECONOMIC VALUE OF YOUR DATA

The final step involves linking the financial value of your new strategy with the data sources and the predictive capabilities necessary to successfully execute each use case. The financial value of each of your new data-driven projects becomes the basis for appraising the supporting data sources and their worth to the business. This valuation will ultimately drive metrics and targets associated with capturing and using this data, allowing you to track the overall success of each data-value capture initiative.

Three areas where data can drive growth

Now that you have a framework, this section is designed to help you identify the areas of your business and the associated data you should be prioritising.

Your business's worth in financial terms is the discounted value of its forecasted cash flows. As Jeff Bezos rightly points out, 'It's the absolute dollar free cash flow per share that you want to maximise.' So, building on this, what data do you have, and what can you do with this data to generate additional future cash flows? Our experience shows there are three primary areas of focus that, if seen to, will ensure future free cash flow:

» improving decision making

» improving operations

» monetising data as a valuable asset.

Figure 4.4 illustrates these areas and their impact on your growth agenda.

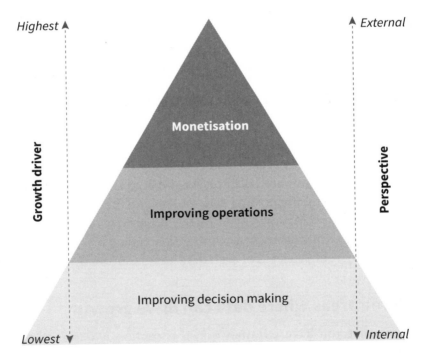

Figure 4.4: the data value pyramid

Before we dive into these three areas, here are two case studies to help contextualise them.

Companies are now being bought and sold based on the value and nature of the data they have. In 2015, IBM announced it was acquiring most of The Weather Company, which owns weather.com and Weather Underground, for a reported US$2 billion. Why? For the company's data. Its weather-related data sets are vast, including data from three billion weather forecast reference points, 50 000 flights and more than 40 million smartphones per day. It's no wonder nearly three-quarters of The Weather Company's scientists are computer and data scientists, while only one-quarter are atmospheric scientists and meteorologists. Now IBM has access to and owns the data, meaning it can monetise it by selling it to companies whose day-to-day activities are impacted by the weather. Weather data has uses well beyond the obvious ones of agriculture and transportation. The weather is known to affect consumer shopping behaviour, employee wellbeing, auction prices and general productivity. We don't yet know what kind of value can be squeezed out of many of these large data sets. For those who know how to interrogate the data, future applications for findings are limited only by the human imagination.

In 2016, Microsoft purchased LinkedIn for US$26.2 billion, giving Microsoft access to LinkedIn's networks of more than 400 million users, as well as the associated data. Let's consider the characteristics of the data Microsoft has acquired and can use. First, there's the fact that the data is time-series based. An individual's activity on LinkedIn (posts, shares, likes, connections, profile updates) changes over time. This can help any business gain insights of a directional nature — an individual's propensity or likelihood to change jobs, for example. This data is also useful in order to target advertising or identify thought leaders who can influence buying patterns.

With a small degree of creativity, it's not hard to see where and how the data can be valuable. Finally, there's the value of LinkedIn data in improving the features and value proposition of Microsoft's existing products, such as Azure, Skype, Office and Outlook.

Both IBM and Microsoft are making significant investments in data, and the underlying infrastructure and skills to leverage this data, allowing these advanced technology companies to take on bigger, more ambitious data projects. If you are only just starting out, from a prioritisation standpoint, you are going to be challenged (and maybe a little overwhelmed). There is an explosion of data available and, through applying some of the ideas in this chapter, you'll have a mass of opportunities to pursue. As tempting as it is to do everything, you're better off picking a few key combinations to ensure you are competitive. Think quality over quantity. With that in mind, here's an outline of three ways you can use data to drive growth.

USING DATA TO IMPROVE DECISION MAKING

You already know that data can help inform better decisions about your business. In this section, we will examine the process of humans interpreting data in order to make better decisions.

There are four key areas of your business where data can improve your decision making: finance, internal operations, people and customers. Determine which of these seems to be underperforming, and define what could be done to improve performance in that area. This may involve a comparison metrics in these areas to an industry benchmark to determine where to focus. Then ask questions that relate to this objective to guide you on where to source the relevant data. If you are looking for a place to start, here are some key areas to consider, along with questions to ask:

» **Predictive maintenance.** What machines are we using? What failures typically occur? What does the failure process look like? What failure indicators exist?

» **Call centre routing.** What do the most frequent calls relate to? Who has the knowledge base to deal with these calls, and where are they located? What information do they need to know to deal with these calls? What is the root cause of these calls?

» **Demand forecasting.** When are our busiest months? What are our most popular items? Where are our bottlenecks in delivering our most popular items? Where is the highest demand for our most popular items?

» **Supply chain optimisation.** Where are our biggest supply chain bottlenecks? Where is our biggest demand? Where are our biggest costs in the supply chain?

» **Fraud or theft identification.** Where in the business are we most susceptible to fraud or theft? What measures do we currently have in place, and are they effective? What are the most common fraud or theft issues in our market sector, and have we accounted for them appropriately?

» **Location or area planning.** Where is the biggest demand for our items? Which areas will drive the biggest growth of our key target market over the next year, five years and ten years? Do we have enough warehouse space to support growth?

» **Employee engagement.** Which division is the most productive? Are our employees happy at work? Is our decision-making process slow and ineffective? Do employees enjoy being at work? Do teams collaborate with one another?

Once you have the necessary data related to your objective, you need a way to identify and then communicate the insights you garner from this data. The good news is that there are now excellent and inexpensive tools that allow you to communicate insights in a more effective way, including Tableau, Microsoft Power BI, Qlik and many others. A spreadsheet is unlikely to be an effective tool, especially if you need to ascertain buy-in from stakeholders, as its visualisation capacity goes only so far.

Don't underestimate the effectiveness of thick data to counterbalance the insights you have gleaned from big data. For example, an organisational transformation may be needed, but if not undertaken properly, it can undermine a company's culture and leave you in a worse off position than when you started. This type of information is more qualitative than quantitative, and is therefore not something your big data would warn you about. You can mitigate this risk by engaging thick-data experts to work alongside you and your leadership team to understand the most effective path forward with respect to your transformation and, where issues may arise, to help ensure success.

As an effective leader, you know the power of storytelling in helping spread lessons quickly throughout your organisation. Balancing thick-data and big-data insights provides a narrative you can use to help share the fact that your insights are grounded and substantiated, taking into account strong data signals, as well as what people feel and perceive.

IMPROVING OPERATIONS

In the previous section, our focus was on how data can help humans make better decisions. Machines, however, can use data to help your business run more efficiently — from the warehouse to recruitment, service delivery, customer services and everything in between. Machine-to-machine communication is a key element of this, and something we will explore further in chapter 6.

As with using data to improve decision making, you need to look at your operations to identify which areas to focus on. Examples include:

» **assortment optimisation.** Software solutions can ensure you have the right goods in the right place through leveraging customer purchasing data.

» **cross- or up-selling.** Software can make tailored recommendations based on the data gathered as customers interact with you.

» **automated stock control.** Warehouse and inventory management solutions track your warehouse inventory in real time, and can reorder when stocks are running low and order more when demand is expected to be higher.

» **fraud detection.** Fraud detection tools can identify malicious anomalies in your data and recommend or automatically implement appropriate responses.

» **predicting customer churn.** Data in customer relationship management (CRM) software can identify patterns in customer behaviours, including historical purchases and last points of engagement, and based on analysis across your whole customer base, correlate certain events with future actions, like defection or negative reviews. With such insight you can set up response systems, for example automatically offering a special deal to recognise loyalty and reduce churn to competitors.

» **dynamic B2C pricing.** Pricing algorithms dynamically change the price of a product or service through leveraging data models based on overall demand.

» **value-based B2B pricing.** Algorithms can change the price of a product or service based on the perceived value of the product or service to the customer.

The best opportunities for data-driven decision making in your business will be a function of your strategic objectives, industry, competition and budget. The key is to think first about the greatest potential ROI, and to couple this with a clear-headed appraisal of your available high-quality data.

MONETISING DATA AS A VALUABLE ASSET

Across an increasing number of industries, there's a growing opportunity to monetise data in a structured and curated form. Quality data sources are hard to come by but increasingly valuable to help enhance artificial intelligence applications or big-data analysis initiatives. Many companies are willing to pay for data sets they deem valuable, and you too have the opportunity to purchase valuable data where it will enhance your organisational objectives. Parameters such as data volume, time series, frequency of access (download) or data granularity can be used to vary subscription characteristics. For example, your company might provide access to a particular data source, including all historical data and with detailed levels of granularity, for a price of $1000 per month, or only current and future data for $500 per month.

Data-as-a-service opportunities can be developed in partnership between public and private organisations. For example, the cloud-based analytics software business Tableau facilitates access to hundreds of third-party data sources that can be examined by licensed users in combination with their own data sets. This service, combined with proprietary data visualisation tools that allow users to commercialise and extend access to the data, have the effect of increasing Tableau's user base and the volume of data available for its subscribers.

Questions

1. Can you use your data to offer new products or services to your existing customers? If so, is it data you can sell, or is it being used to increase the overall value of your products or services?

2. Can you leverage data to serve new customers who are currently not served by you or your competitors?

3. How central is data to your current or future competitive advantage?

4. What is the best way to collect thick data, taking into account the time and resources required?

5. What benefits could you gain by talking to your teams about integrating big-data and thick-data approaches to realising data value?

6. Where do you see opportunities to flip the standard approach on its head, so your managers' subjective assessments are incorporated into data-driven analyses, rather than the reverse?

7. What data do you have already, and how can you leverage it to open up new opportunities and revenue streams?

8. Do your current teams have a digital-first and data-driven mindset? If they did, how different would your situation be?

Chapter summary

There has been an explosion of data, and this is only set to increase. The giants of big tech have mined for and consumed data to successfully power their economic engines. A number of pre-digital incumbents have caught on, realising just how powerful proprietary data is. Now it's your turn to do the same. You should now have a clear understanding of the value of data, what it can be used for, where to find it and how to extract value.

In this chapter we also discussed the concept of thick data, which is data that focuses on the qualitative rather than the quantitative. Thick data will be a powerful tool in better serving your customers, as well as ensuring you're getting the most out of your employees. Big data without thick data really only tells half the story.

The application of data in your business is critical in our new economy. Our five-step framework will help you identify opportunities for the use of data in your business and will effectively tie these back to your strategies for success, as discussed in chapter 1. You should also consider the nature of your data investment — whether it is data to improve decision making or enhance your operations, or data you can monetise or sell. The latter is what underpins many of the valuations supporting the largest and most dominant companies in the world. If they can do it, so can you.

In chapter 5, we turn our attention to platforms, including analysing the digital platforms of the top tech companies.

CHAPTER 5
Platforms

Commerce changes the fate and
genius of nations.
Thomas Gray

The tectonic plates of big business have shifted. Now, the most successful companies in the world have a digital platform at their core. Facebook, Alibaba, Google, Amazon — they all have one, and so should you.

Platforms provide value for all users as they are able to share resources. The economic value, however, comes to those who own the platform and facilitate exchanges that would not otherwise occur. The more transactions you expedite, the more money you generate. Being the platform provider also minimises your exposure to risk, which is dispersed among all the platform's contributors and users. And the beauty of enabling all these interactions and innovations is data. Platforms naturally attract data. Data drives informed decision making, providing the platform owner with insights into future trends, opportunities and of course new cash streams. If you think that sounds like a flywheel, you'd be right.

Breaking these concepts down into first principles, we can see how a platform generates value through facilitating transactions. A shopping centre is a pre-digital platform (see figure 5.1); it has suppliers (the shops) and it has buyers. The platform owner provides infrastructure such as cleaning, power, toilets, parking and so on, which not only complements the transactions, but actually facilitates said transactions by improving the shopping experience. Thanks to the infrastructure and amenities of the shopping centre, shop owners profit from happy customers, but of course the real value comes from owning the shopping centre — the platform — and fostering the shopping ecosystem.

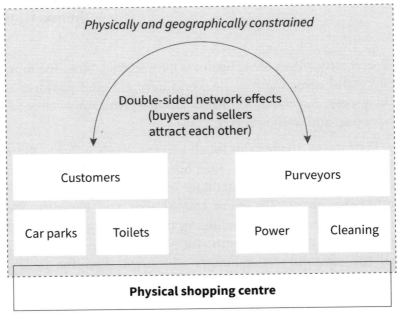

Figure 5.1: the pre-digital platform (shopping centre)

A digital platform (see figure 5.2) is based on the same premise as a shopping centre, except it offers a plethora of new opportunities. For instance, a shopping centre is limited by physical and cost constraints. It can only penetrate a local market, meaning its growth is limited, or at least expensive. A digital platform, on the other hand, isn't geographically constrained. Customers and third-party sellers can be located anywhere in the world, so new and unique interactions can be created that would never have occurred previously.

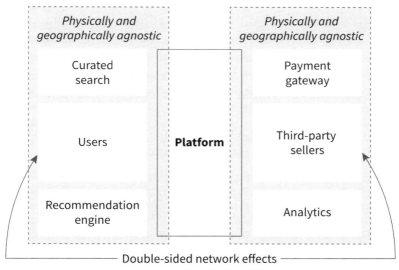

Figure 5.2: the digital platform

Apple is a prime example of a digital platform business. Its platform is iOS, which allows third-party companies to connect to customers by building and selling apps on the iPhone and iPad. The apps increase the overall value of these mobile devices, without Apple having to invest additional resources. Further, for each app sale, Apple claims 30 cents per dollar. So, by providing a platform, Apple is able to ensure new value is continuously being created for the user in the form of iPhone and iPad apps, while profiting from all sales and completely avoiding the development risk. This effectively generates free cash flow. In contrast, most pre-digital incumbents are pipeline businesses, where value is created as resources flow down the supply chain from producer to consumer.

Crucially, a platform business does not control value creation. It creates the infrastructure and tools to enable value creation. Digital platforms facilitate new interactions and new innovations, as well as substituting antiquated processes at price points that in the past would have been considered impossible. Platforms also connect businesses that traditionally would have been competitors, providing companies with access to new market segments. The possibilities for value creation are endless when applied within the context of a platform business.

This chapter will help you understand platforms and put in place a strategy to apply this theory to your own organisation. Most companies will never become solely a platform company, but there are elements of a platform you can employ to create an ecosystem around your products, increasing margins and introducing new revenue streams.

The network effect of platforms

Platforms are, at their most basic level, a conduit to connect buyers and sellers with one another. Nobody wants to join a platform on which they are unable to transact, but people do want to join a platform where there are lots of other people to transact with. So, as platforms grow, their value and their 'pull' increases. This is known as Metcalfe's Law, according to which a good or service increases in value exponentially as more people use it. For your business, this can be a powerful profit generator. Right now, you are probably limited in the money you can make with the resources you own and the way you allocate them. A platform, on the other hand, is only limited by the resources, decisions and imaginations of its contributors, which, in theory, could be endless. Bill Gates once said, 'A platform is when the economic value of everybody that uses it exceeds the value of the company that creates it. Then it's a platform.' In other words, the platform becomes more valuable than the organisation that owns it (a concept your accountant might struggle with!).

When a platform hits a critical mass of users, the value offered outweighs the cost of joining and a network effect is created. Before this tipping point, you need to find some other incentive for parties to join your platform. Keep this in mind as you develop a business plan and start setting expectations.

The platform network effect is closely linked to the concept of demand- and supply-side economics discussed in chapter 1: scale itself creates value. The landline telephone is the classic one-sided network where there is only one type of user. As the number of telephone users grows, the value of the network grows, attracting more users, creating a virtuous cycle. In contrast, a marketplace, like the shopping centre, is two-sided — there are merchants and buyers. Having more shopfronts attracts foot traffic, while more shoppers attracts merchants. This phenomenon, in which the value for one group is defined by the size of the other group(s), is called cross-sided network effects. As you can see in figure 5.3 (overleaf), this again creates a virtuous cycle. Platforms can have more than two user groups, and the relationships between these groups can become complicated, but the principles stay the same. Note that these user groups will have different wants and needs with respect to platform functionality and capabilities.

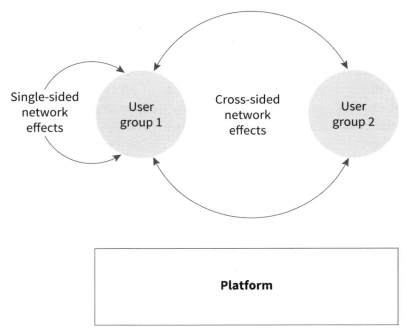

Figure 5.3: platform network effects

It's important to note that simply creating the platform is no guarantee of success. Let's look at the dominant online marketplace for short-term holiday rentals, Airbnb, and its battle with a lesser known competitor. Early on in Airbnb's life, it came up against a European rival named Wimdu. At the time, Airbnb had a strong US presence but a significantly smaller footprint in Europe. Wimdu had just raised $90 million and was primed to take the European market, which would position it well for global domination. Airbnb responded quickly and aggressively. After all, there is only one global market, and Europe is a major key to controlling that market. Within three months, it had 'localised' Airbnb, making the website more accessible for European visitors by incorporating language and cultural adaptations and opening eight offices in Europe. By moving faster than its competitors, Airbnb was able to take hold of the European market, controlling both Europe and the United States, and creating a global network. Although Wimdu started with a similar capital base, it was unable to keep pace with Airbnb's market share capture.

Later in this chapter, we explain how to transition (at least partially) from a pipeline to a platform business. But first we'll present a platform 'crash course' of sorts. In the following section, we reveal what is driving the platform era, and the first two types of platform companies. We also discuss the power of aggregation, and the importance of complements and openness.

A platform crash course

The network effect of platforms has brought with it a new economic model that has disrupted, and is disrupting, a plethora of industries. Pre-digital incumbents have risen to power through leveraging economies of scale, or supply-side scale, while the most powerful tech giants (like Facebook, Amazon and now even General Electric) are leveraging network effects, or, in economic terms, demand-side economies of scale. So what is driving the platform era? Basically, the same things that drove the digital era: cloud computing, better computing power, mobile devices and networks. These technologies have allowed people and objects to connect with one another in real time regardless of geographic location. Coupled with the internet, they have also enabled the free transmission of information and made it available anywhere in the world almost instantly.

Platforms are also powerful in their ability to reduce the incremental costs associated with selling a good or service.

In any business, these marginal costs can be broken down as follows:

1. **marginal costs of production** — the cost of producing one more item

2. **distribution costs** — the cost of shipping an item to the customer or provisioning a service

3. **transaction costs** — the cost of executing a transaction for a good or service.

If you have a platform, marginal costs associated with replication and distribution are almost zero. While only a handful of platform companies are able to reduce all three of these costs to close to zero, many have been able to lower one or two to close to zero, which still provides a fantastic competitive advantage.

The devastating effect of bringing down marginal costs to close to zero is that the (supply-side) economies of scale pre-digital incumbents used to cement their position no longer provide a competitive advantage. This is especially true for information-based businesses like publishing or advertising. For instance, to create and distribute a magazine requires staff, a printing press, distribution channels and seller relationships. The barriers to entry to starting an offline magazine are massive because profitability depends on selling large quantities, leveraging economies of scale. To start a magazine today is extremely expensive, and it becomes profitable (maybe) only at scale. In the digital world, these barriers don't exist, as information is freely replicable and distributable, globally accessible and on demand — all at the touch of a button.

THE BIRTH OF PLATFORM COMPANIES

The first set of platform companies took full advantage of their primacy in the market, creating new forums for information and data exchange, such as social media platforms, online news platforms and music streaming services. These models did away with traditional value chains creating physical goods and singular services. For instance, music streaming services unbundled individual songs from the tangible CD, integrating music with mobile devices. They aggregated a vast amount of music, making individual songs available on demand, and, interestingly, re-bundled songs into playlists for different artists, genres and so on, creating an entirely new way for customers to consume music at any time, from anywhere (as long as they had a mobile device).

The second iteration of platforms blended the offline with the online, commonly known as online to offline (O2O) platforms. Network effects and near-zero marginal costs were applied to the offline world by leveraging digital technologies that handled huge amounts of data and information, from transactional and pricing data to user preferences — all for an extremely low cost. These digital platforms were created to manage and connect the physical world, creating new interactions and transactions on a global scale that simply could not have occurred in the past. In many cases, the relationship the platform owners have with the physical world is unique, in that they can decouple themselves from owning the tangible asset, and focus on providing value to the customer by facilitating and fostering relationships rather than trying to create it all themselves.

Examples of this have occurred in numerous industries, Airbnb and Uber being two notable disruptors. Airbnb has decoupled rooms from trusted hotel brands, and Uber has decoupled vehicles from trusted taxi companies. In both these examples, the physical asset was modularised and commoditised, and effectively outsourced to third parties. Initially, these physical goods were a constraint, as to scale meant investing in expensive infrastructure and assets. These organisations were able to do this by creating a trusted platform that aggregated the spare rooms and empty cars within a city.

As their networks grow, these companies can add more rooms or cars to their platforms without having to physically invest in additional rooms or cars. It's important to note that investment is still required to build their networks (when Uber moves into another city, it requires new offices and infrastructure), and some costs, such as regulatory checks, will never disappear. But eventually, in theory, the network effect will reach a certain point at which the network pulls in users organically, and the investment required to grow the network becomes negligible compared with the size of the user base. This is the potential power of demand-side economies of scale.

THE POWER OF AGGREGATION

Ben Thompson, founder of the tech newsletter *Stratechery*, has coined the term *aggregation theory* to explain what happens when suppliers are co-located and the costs associated with matching suppliers with buyers are naturally lowered. These are effectively two- (or more) sided platforms that own the relationship between supplier and buyer. For instance, food delivery companies such as UberEats and Deliveroo have aggregated thousands of restaurants across hundreds of cities, creating a significantly better customer experience for the user. Therefore, controlling demand and in-turn, the relationship between the user and restaurants. To be classified as a true platform aggregator puts you in the same league as Facebook, Uber, Airbnb and Netflix — it is the ultimate platform play.

When a platform is an aggregator, all three of the marginal costs mentioned earlier (on the supply side) will be equal to or close to zero. This is because the platform facilitates the sale and distribution of digital information or goods, which is extremely cheap to do, especially at scale. The digital good may represent a physical object; nonetheless, the marginal cost incurred by the platform owner to provide it is negligible, as they are only dealing with the digital aspect of this trade. Transaction costs and distribution costs are either pushed onto the suppliers or consumers, or automated away. This means that for a platform aggregator, scaling is extremely cheap and easy to do. Further, to be an aggregator, the platform must have commoditised supply, meaning direct control over inventory, even if it does not directly own it. This is because suppliers agree to join the platform on the terms defined by the platform aggregator, as there are numerous end users willing and wanting to buy. The main takeaway is that platform aggregators should focus on the demand side of the platform first — that is, getting lots of end users. Suppliers are always attracted to where there is demand.

This leads into another important aspect of aggregation theory that is applicable to all companies. The owners of the platform aren't constrained by traditional supplier agreements or by owning physical assets, though some may choose to do so for a variety of reasons. Because of this, they are free to focus on the users and can dedicate resources to creating a fantastic user experience through things like discovery and curation tools, and by making it extremely easy for new users to join on both the demand and the supply side of the platform.

Through curating great experiences, platform aggregators control demand. If you control demand, then suppliers will flock to your platform. Most platforms sealed their success by offering a better experience than anything else on the market, by focusing on a different section of the value chain and by application of the conservation of attractive profits — think Amazon.

Ben Thompson describes three levels of platform providers that are based around the platform provider's relationship to the suppliers and the costs they endure through ascertaining supply:

1. **Supply acquisition aggregator.** Level one platform aggregators pay for their supply. Their market power stems from their superior buying power

through controlling demand (a function of being an aggregator). This means supply is limited to the resources available to a level one aggregator, hence they take longer to build. Netflix, for example, pays for content, including the unique content it shows.

2. **Supply transaction cost aggregator.** Level two platform aggregators do not pay for supply, though they do incur transaction costs in bringing suppliers onto their platform. For instance, Uber has to pay for regulatory checks every time it recruits a new driver. This limits supply growth, though to a lesser degree than for level one aggregators.

3. **Zero supply cost aggregator.** Level three platform aggregators do not pay for supply or incur any costs in acquiring suppliers. This means there are zero marginal costs associated with supply and demand, so through owning the relationship between the two parties, they are able to profit from the relationship without incurring any costs. Only a handful of platform companies enjoy this sort of business nirvana. Google is a level three aggregator, as its users generate and consume content. Level three aggregators typically incorporate a third user group, such as advertisers, to drive revenue, as the platform is typically free for the other user groups (which ensures frictionless scaling).

It should be noted that though platform aggregators have no marginal costs on the demand side, and significantly lower costs on the supply side, they will most likely have large fixed costs, such as the costs of their software, and, over a long timeframe, all fixed costs become variable costs. That said, as these platforms grow their respective user groups, these costs are spread across the users until they are significantly small, especially once the network effect comes into play and the platform 'pull' attracts new users organically.

COMPLEMENTS AND OPENNESS

The last part of our platform crash course relates to complements. Complements are defined as goods or services for which the decrease in the price (or increased availability) of one good or service increases demand for the paired good or service. In the world of platforms, this concept is extremely powerful. The Apple iPhone is a great example of using complements to increase the value and hence the demand for a platform. Apple enabled app developers to build applications on the iPhone. Apple does not pay for these applications. In fact, it makes a profit from them. But the iPhone without these apps is significantly less valuable to the user. These applications are not only a great way for Apple to increase the demand for its applications dramatically, but they're also a fantastic revenue earner, as discussed earlier in this chapter.

There are many forms of complements. In the platform world, complements are usually included for free or outsourced to third parties, as in Apple's strategy. What Apple does do, though, is supply the (free) tools to developers to make it easier for them to build on the Apple platform. Effectively, then, Apple provides the developers with the necessary free tools (a supply-side complement) to create applications (a demand-side complement) for iPhone users. It's important to highlight here that complements differ for the user groups if you're running a multi-sided platform, as different user groups have different wants and needs.

With every digital transaction, there is information to be collected and insight to be gained. As discussed in chapter 4, time-based data series provide rich insights into your user groups, allowing you to spot and even pre-empt trends, needs and issues that arise. This is why owning the platform is so important — it's the ultimate data honey trap. Through owning the platform, you have access to the data of your end consumers and the suppliers, as well as any other party that engages with the platform, giving you a holistic view of your ecosystem. Leveraging the data allows platform owners to optimise the core interactions taking place on the platform and the associated user experience. This can include enhancing the platform's matchmaking capabilities, improving curation, or providing toolkits, help guides, analytics or human expertise.

The right complements for any platform depend on the platform itself. What's important to remember is how you offer these complements. — what can you give away for free or at a low price that will increase demand for your platform? And what can you get users to pay for that will increase demand for your platform? You may even want to outsource the creation of platform complements to third parties. How you choose to price your complements can significantly change the demand for your platform. Whatever you choose, trying to get people to pay for something they initially had for free is a near impossible job, so make sure you have done your homework and analysed the data.

Closely linked to complements is openness, which defines the extent to which third parties can innovate and create value on your platform. The iPhone wouldn't be as valuable as it is today if Apple hadn't allowed third-party app developers to build novel applications that leveraged Apple's integrated hardware and software. Some pundits argue that Apple still doesn't provide enough flexibility for these app builders and that more value could be unlocked, but doing so would mean Apple loses control around things like quality and customer experience. The openness debate relates to control. To open up your platform entirely, which is effectively what open-source software does (as discussed further in chapter 8), means losing control and profits, and profiting in the world of open source is extremely challenging. If you wish to own the platform, therefore, it is imperative that you control the core functionality and features that create the most value for your users. To reap the maximum benefit from your platform, you must own the value-adding components, whether this means buying valuable new additions created by users or building them yourself.

From pipeline to platform

Most of the companies discussed in this chapter were born digital. They started out as a platform company, or at least set the foundations from the very beginning to become a platform company. For a pre-digital incumbent, this is certainly not the case, and to build a platform business requires a whole new strategy and culture.

If you're going to introduce a platform strategy into your business, you must be willing to open up to the world, and this includes competitors. Transparency, openness, sharing and community are key factors that drive successful platform companies. The goal is to create more than you capture.

If you want to leverage network effects and zero marginal costs, the first step is to figure out how you can create new relationships and interactions that unlock new forms of value. There is a common misconception that implementing a platform strategy will save a failing business. This is incorrect. If you're going to build a platform out of a pipeline business, then you have to start with a good product, one that relates to your core strategy and customer engagement.

As a pre-digital incumbent, you have been leveraging supply-side economies of scale to distribute your IP to your customers at a low price point. This approach doesn't suddenly become obsolete in the digital age. You can leverage the relationships you have with your customers, as well as your domain expertise, to create new and novel interactions, which you can then build your platform around.

This is where your Engine B plays an important role. Consolidate your core activities and build out digital channels to reach your current clients, as well as future clients. These digital endeavours need to be centralised, ensuring that the data is also centralised and accessible. Your employees need to be working side by side rather than focusing on disparate digital initiatives. From here it's about creating an ecosystem and opening up your pipeline to new players. In the next three sections, we'll show you how to build, manage and measure the success of your new platform.

Building the platform

One of the most effective ways to implement a platform strategy is to open up your customer base to third-party sellers, allowing them to provide goods or services that complement your core offering. This involves creating a hybrid business model that blends a product and platform strategy. For many pipeline businesses this may seem counterintuitive, as it effectively means not only connecting potential competitors with your customers, but also granting them access to your data and IP. It's important to remember that the platform world is based on trust and transparency. Many pipeline businesses struggle with this concept, as value creation is a tug of war between competitors. In the platform world, value creation goes well beyond the means of a single entity, as network effects and zero marginal costs come into play.

For instance, in late 2017, Macquarie Bank launched its devXchange platform, which allows third parties to interact with data stored in Macquarie's core transaction systems via application program interfaces, or APIs (code that allows two software programs to communicate with each other). This means that Macquarie customers can move seamlessly between financial applications and banking products to find the solutions that best meet their needs. For third parties, it means they suddenly have access to a huge ecosystem of clients and financial data, providing them with the necessary tools to build new and better financial applications. Macquarie has created a two-sided platform by opening up its customers to third parties. John Deere has done the same, opening up the data collected from all its machinery to both farmers and agriculture software providers. John Deere provides the necessary tools (complements) to make this a frictionless and seamless experience.

Notice here that in both cases the third parties are primarily focused on developing software complements. This is very similar to the Apple model, where Apple owns the tangible good and incurs marginal costs in providing said good. But it also allows third parties to enhance the product through building complementary apps, where Apple does not incur any marginal costs in providing these complements to the end customer, or with respect to bringing in new developers. Similarly, both John Deere and Macquarie own the relationship with the end customer, and don't actually incur any marginal costs in providing the user with access to the digital complements that these third parties are building on top of their primary offerings. Just like Apple, John Deere and Macquarie are leveraging supply- and demand-side economies of scale, which makes for a truly powerful moat.

Both are great examples of opening up a customer base to third-party sellers, creating new value for customers and third-party groups through strengthening the value proposition of a good or service. This is a great approach for traditional pipeline companies because it helps them transition away from a product or service mindset to a platform mindset. So rather than just focusing on creating a more differentiated product or service compared with your competitors, you can foster new interactions and create an ecosystem around your goods or services, which you can control and profit from. The beauty of this is that your company can adopt more of a platform model without neglecting your current customers.

As a pre-digital incumbent, no doubt you have some sort of value chain, coupled with disparate distribution channels — most likely including some sort of digital element — and siloed data stores. We're guessing your business looks something like figure 5.4.

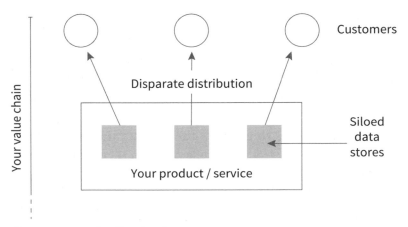

Figure 5.4: a pipeline business

To successfully introduce a platform, you need to take a systematic approach. First, begin to create a community around your core product. Bring customers together and ensure that having them connect with one another is a valuable experience for all. Provide them with tight feedback channels direct to your team(s), collect data around them to understand their needs, work with them to identify new opportunities for your products, and make changes accordingly. It's imperative that you shift your focus away from the bottom line and onto your customers.

This first stage represents the initialisation of your Engine B, as discussed in chapter 2, which allows for a more agile and iterative approach to meeting the needs of your customers, as well as ensuring you have a centralised body building out your digital platform. Far from being neglected, the core units of your Engine A are still running, and their staff are both required and valued as they bring a wealth of experience and knowledge. However, when you choose to kick-start your platform, it is important that it's centralised, coordinated, agile and digitally driven — you want to ensure you can leverage the world of zero cost distribution.

What you've done here is to prime the demand side of your platform, which organically fuels your digital transformation. Customers are interacting with you and themselves in new ways. You're enhancing your current offering, and building out new products based on your customers' feedback and the data you are collecting. In short, your ecosystem is becoming much more open and collaborative. Further, the digital aspect of your offerings and your digital channels are centralised and share common features. Figure 5.5 suggests how your business should now look.

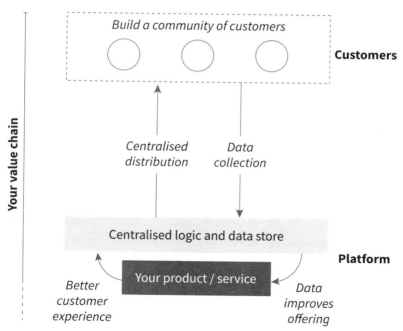

Figure 5.5: a single-sided platform

The next stage is to introduce third parties to build complementary products alongside your core offering, creating more value for your customers and increasing the 'stickiness' of your platform. This is when double-sided network effects come into play, as third parties attract customers and customers attract third parties. As shown by Macquarie, John Deere and Apple, the best complement to a tangible good or manual service is software — think zero marginal costs. So ensure these third parties are leveraging your data and building out digital complements. You also need to begin focusing on managing the new relationships that arise through bringing third parties onto the platform. No longer is it just you and your customers; now you need to ensure that both parties are benefiting equally from each other. A major caveat here is that if you let the wrong third parties onto your platform, your customers may very well associate a bad experience with your platform and brand. To ensure you are letting only the right third parties onto your platform, we recommend creating mandatory guidelines and service-level agreements for third parties that are aligned to your operating model and platform vision. At this stage, your business probably looks something like figure 5.6.

The last stage is to fully embrace the hybrid model. This requires shifting more resources to building out the infrastructure and tools that can optimise the interactions occurring on your platform. This stage requires a strong focus on your data to gain better insights into your user groups, building — or allowing third parties to build — complements on both the demand and the supply side to drive demand-side economies of scale, and optimising your user experience for frictionless interactions. Remember, an aggregator always controls the relationship with the end customer, because if you control demand, then you control supply. Therefore, ensuring the quality of these interactions is essential if you want your platform to grow in size and reach. You must make sure you implement the appropriate governance to enforce quality for the end customer, while making the ecosystem flexible enough to allow for innovation and new forms of value creation. This relates to the openness of your platform, as discussed earlier in this chapter. There's a fine line between platform growth and stagnation.

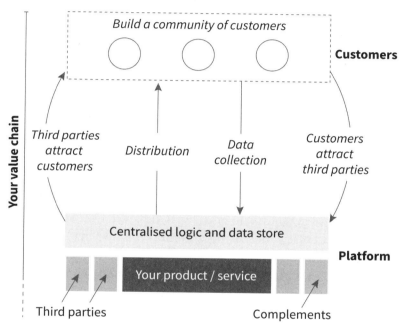

Figure 5.6: a double-sided platform

What we have just discussed is an effective approach designed to guide any pre-digital incumbent through building a platform around its core products. Whether or not you go beyond the hybrid model to become an entirely platform-driven organisation will really depend on your situation and strategy. There are also other approaches that a pipeline business can take to building a platform, such as connecting two customer groups that typically connect outside of your offering, or creating an offering for your customers' customers and then connecting the two. Both are valid options. However, we champion the hybrid approach as being the most accessible of the three, as the other two require specific groups of customers and specific strategic objectives, which most companies don't have.

Before we go on, you may have noticed that building a platform is very similar to building your flywheel. That's because the platform is actually the foundation to any successful flywheel as it's the conduit that connects you to your customers and third parties, as well as third parties to your customers — network effects are critical in ensuring your flywheel spins. The platform also plays a vital role in collecting and using data to improve the overall customer experience.

Managing inside out

The value of a platform goes well beyond the boundaries of a single entity. Fostering interactions and having users contribute to the overall value creates an entirely new operating model, one that looks out rather than in. If you want to create a platform that leverages the growth of network effects, then you need to focus on your wider environment, and identify opportunities that enable new forms of interactions and transactions.

Perspective is everything. A traditional pipeline business will focus on internal efficiencies, internal research and development, internal resources and the internal value created for the external customer. In doing so, the business creates a barrier between itself and the environment beyond, with company culture following suit. To benefit from the compounding growth effects of a successful platform, you need to change this perspective. This involves three shifts.

1. RESOURCE ORCHESTRATION

Instead of looking to control resources, create an environment where third parties can utilise each other's resources to generate new goods and services. Platform value is produced through a number of different parties working together to create value well beyond what they could achieve by themselves.

A quirky example of resource orchestration is Reddit, a social news aggregator. Reddit users share their experiences and knowledge with one another to create value for all involved.

2. CREATION TO FACILITATION

The key to a successful platform is its ability to spur interactions while maintaining platform liquidity. This is all about fostering the right ecosystem, and putting in place the right checks and balances to ensure quality interactions and transactions. As the owner of the platform, it is your job to ensure the right parties are interacting with one another, and that interactions are as trustworthy and as seamless as possible.

For instance, virtually all social platforms like Facebook and LinkedIn recommend new friends and people to follow based on your current friends and how you interact with the platform.

3. ECOSYSTEM VALUE

It's essential to remember that the platform ecosystem is extremely dynamic, so you need to ensure the infrastructure and governance — designed to facilitate quality interactions — continue to evolve. Implementing feedback loops and leveraging collected data will drive your platform's roadmap. A critical part of the continual improvement of your platform is giving all members a voice. This creates a community rather than a dictatorship, encouraging parties to participate and create. Remember, platforms are all about creating more value than you capture, so don't get greedy.

An extreme case is open-source software projects where the project's roadmap is dictated by the members of the project. For instance, Ethereum, which is an open-source software platform based on blockchain technology, allows users to build entire revenue-making applications on the Ethereum blockchain. A blockchain is a decentralised and immutable ledger or database of transactions that occur on a network. It is the underlying technology that enables modern cryptocurrencies such as Bitcoin. Users can choose to build on the public Ethereum blockchain or create their own for private use. Though there is a not-for-profit organisation called the Ethereum Foundation developing the base code, anyone can download the necessary tools to build applications on the Ethereum blockchain. The Ethereum Foundation does not profit from people building on the Ethereum blockchain, as it is only there to oversee the development of Ethereum and build the Ethereum community. Because of this, the Ethereum community has a strong influence on the overall development of Ethereum.

To truly leverage the power of the platform, you need to focus your attention outward, on your customer and the world around you. This requires a cultural change and a strategy change, focusing on collaboration rather than competition. The leadership team has to shift its focus to the management of externalities. There is a change from overarching control to the collection and orchestration of resources and people that move and interact on your platform. The company no longer has to focus on seizing every opportunity that presents itself. Instead, management should focus on only the best opportunities, while aiding platform partners to seize the remaining opportunities, ensuring the platform as a whole is as strong as possible.

Measuring success

To ensure platform growth, the metrics you use to measure growth also have to change. Most likely, your metrics focus solely on how quickly value flows through the pipeline. Platform metrics must track how value is created for all users, which encourages the continual growth of positive network effects.

What creates value for your users? It's the interactions that are enabled by your platform. So the metrics you create must focus on increasing and optimising these interactions. For example, LinkedIn measures the time you spend on its app, as well as your interactions and preferences, helping drive the effectiveness for advertisers. Trust is also imperative. For example, Uber and Airbnb are worth nothing if suppliers do not trust them, or the platform users, so trust must be built and sustained if a platform is to grow.

It's important to note that when starting out, you should limit your platform to one type of interaction. Ensure you do it extremely well, and build the foundations before you scale. As an example, Amazon started by selling books. Now it sells a huge assortment of items, builds hardware products and runs Amazon Web Services, another platform in itself! This was only possible through starting small, and putting in place the right culture and organisational design to ensure Amazon was able to grow into the behemoth we know today. Amazon has always championed an extremely customer-centric model, with a primary focus on fulfilment, arrival times, minimising returns, seller feedback, seller stock management and so on. Every single one of those metrics focuses on the transactions that Amazon facilitates, and on ensuring those transactions have the best possible outcome for all parties involved. Because of this, Amazon's customers trust Amazon, as well as the suppliers that use the Amazon platform.

Questions

1. Is your culture and strategy externally focused, and have you maximised opportunities to collaborate and create new forms of value?

2. Are you focused on collaboration or competition?

3. What is your core product(s) and can you create an ecosystem around it through connecting people or groups?

4. Is there an opportunity to open up your customer base to third parties to provide complements to your core product?

5. Are there things you can give away to create more demand for your platform or product?

6. What would 'success' look like for a platform in your industry?

7. Are you ensuring that you are facilitating and sharing value creation?

8. Are you focusing only on the core needs of your customers and allowing third parties to focus on the long tail of value creation?

Chapter summary

Digital platforms are at the core of our hyper-connected world, leveraging the internet's ability to reproduce digital information at practically no marginal cost, and disrupting traditional incumbents that created empires according to the laws of economies of scale. We have never had so much opportunity at our fingertips. The rise of digital has enabled people to transact with one another as never before, creating new communities that generate ever more value as they grow in size. Individuals, organisations and countries that previously were unable to play on the global stage suddenly have a plethora of channels to create, communicate and profit, financially and otherwise. This new reality doesn't mean pre-digital incumbents are destined for failure. On the contrary, the strategies and tactics used by digital platform companies can be applied equally to traditional pipeline businesses.

The most important parallel between physical and online platforms is that they both foster transactions and leverage network effects. So, when designing your platform, don't think about technology first. Go back to basics and think about the customer — think about the core transactions that you can or want to facilitate. Then figure out how you can enable and optimise these transactions through leveraging technology. Lastly, never forget that you must create more than you capture, for that is where the power of the platform lies.

As the leader of a traditional pipeline business, you can harness the power of network effects and minimised marginal costs through first focusing on your customers. Then, you should focus on creating a more collaborative and communal environment where value is created for your customers as the customer group grows in size — the makings of a one-sided platform. Adding third parties into the mix can provide complements to the core offering, creating new value for all.

Next comes the transition from an internal to an external mindset. Quality transactions for platform users will become an important part of the company's focus. Quality will work hand in hand with trust to promote a core offering that continues to thrive and improve on the back of a hybrid business model that incorporates both pipeline and platform strategy. The hybrid business model will play an integral role in ensuring your flywheel spins with the power of network effects and data.

Now that we've covered data and platforms, which can be viewed as the digital fuel and infrastructure, respectively, of your organisation, the missing part of the stack is the clever engineering. This is where the concept of a *system of intelligence* comes into play. Intelligent algorithms powered by AI and fuelled by data will sit on top of your platform, continually learning from, and optimising the experiences of, those who interact with it. Systems of intelligence are the perfect supplement to your platform, unlocking even more value on both the supply and demand side of your digital ecosystem. We'll discuss this concept in detail in chapter 6.

CHAPTER 6
Systems of intelligence

The object of all work is production or accomplishment and to either of these ends there must be forethought, system, planning, intelligence, and honest purpose, as well as perspiration.
Thomas Edison

For over a decade, big-tech companies have invested heavily in artificial intelligence (AI), and numerous pre-digital incumbents are starting to do the same. There is a shared belief between researchers and business leaders that artificial intelligence will open the door to fantastic growth opportunities, and we agree, but with a caveat. Pursuing artificial intelligence for the sake of it is a dangerous route to take, as it will be filled with wastefulness and disappointment. In many cases, it seems that these investments are technology led, meaning the implementation of artificial intelligence is itself the primary concern, rather than the business outcome. Investing in technology must be business led, not technology led, and artificial intelligence is no exception. Throwing artificial intelligence at everything, or 'AI washing', won't solve all your problems. You need a well-defined business case. Also, before making an investment in artificial intelligence, you need to understand the technology and its potential, and, more importantly, its limitations.

Artificial intelligence is software and can be broken down into two overarching categories: weak and strong artificial intelligence. Weak artificial intelligence is software that can undertake one specific task as well as, or better than, a human. It is designed specifically for that one task and will therefore fail miserably if applied to something else. Strong artificial intelligence is as smart as, or smarter than, a human across the board and can self-teach. This is the kind of artificial intelligence you see in the *Terminator* movies. Strong artificial intelligence doesn't exist yet. But weak artificial intelligence does, and this is what we will be focusing on in this chapter.

Artificial intelligence will eventually permeate all industries. However, as we discussed in chapter 1, on its own it does not provide a point of difference. To realise the growth benefits of artificial intelligence, it must be considered in a systems context, or what we call a *system of intelligence*. A system of intelligence consists of an algorithm (a process or set of rules to be followed in calculations or other problem-solving operations) that provides the 'smarts', the necessary computer processing power and a fantastic user experience. All of this can combine to produce tangible business benefits, such as examining thousands of contracts then extracting key clauses, helping researchers unlock new insights from massive data sets or managing the power usage of large buildings. In this chapter, we discuss the key components of a system of intelligence, starting with machine learning. We also reveal five crucial factors in the successful application of AI and present a range of ideas on how to construct a highly defensible digital moat.

The rise of machine learning

Machine learning gives systems the ability to learn and improve automatically without being explicitly programmed. It is based on the principles of how a child learns — through experience, repetition and, in most cases, feedback. There are three broad categories of machine learning: supervised, unsupervised and reinforcement learning. Machine learning has actually been around since the 1950s but has only recently begun to take centre stage, as the algorithms that fall under the machine learning heading have become layered, allowing them to crunch more information than ever before, which has led to the rise of deep learning (a subset of machine learning that examines computer algorithms that learn and improve on their own).

While much traditional data science focuses on explaining the past, machine learning focuses on explaining what will happen in the future. Simply, machine learning algorithms identify patterns within large data sets and, given a detected pattern, perform an action or produce an output. The real art comes from applying the right machine learning technique to the right data. Machine learning is nothing without data. As more data is fed in, machine learning algorithms are able to continually refine their ability to make predictions, increasing their accuracy and precision. Understanding the data you have, and the problem you want to solve, will in turn dictate the techniques, tools and algorithms you use. The overall goal of machine learning is to create intelligent programs, often called agents, which at their core consist of algorithms that learn and evolve. As already noted, there are three broad categories of machine learning.

SUPERVISED LEARNING

The agent is trained using massive data sets that consist of examples of the correct answer to a particular problem. As data is fed in, the algorithm teaches itself how to infer the desired output given a specified input. The more training data the algorithm is fed, the more accurate the agent's inference capabilities become. It is important to note that the training data is labelled, making it easier for the algorithm to 'learn'. Once the agent is adequately trained, and provided with similar input data, it will classify the data as it was trained to, hopefully producing the desired output. Issues arise when the data used for training doesn't represent the real world or contains biases that can have detrimental consequences. For instance, using historical data to create the algorithms that determine credit rating scores may give white males a better credit rating score compared with females or people of non-Caucasian background, because historically the employment market, and therefore income and ability to maintain strong credit, prejudicially favoured white males. Historical data sets can be riddled with human biases, which can lead the agent to make unfair or erroneous decisions. Although the agent may seem smart, it is only as intelligent as the data you feed it, and any human biases within the training data will flow through into its decision making.

UNSUPERVISED LEARNING

In this case, the agent is given unlabelled data and no defined desired output (unlike supervised learning, where the outcome is defined during the agent's training). As data is fed into the agent, it makes its own classifications and mappings, attempting to cluster the data into similar buckets. The agent is given the freedom to find hidden patterns in the data without being given any direction. As in supervised learning, the data plays an integral role in the patterns the agent detects. This can lead to some very interesting insights. For example, online user behaviour can be monitored by the agent, which will learn over time what 'normal' user behaviour looks like, then be able to identify potential cyber threats by detecting abnormal behaviours. If, say, the agent picks up a log-on from a location that has never before been used by a user of the application, this may prompt the agent to issue a warning notification to the user or to shut down the account, depending on the nature of the application.

REINFORCEMENT LEARNING

Reinforcement learning agents actually mimic the way in which animals and humans learn. The agent is trained by receiving instant feedback on how it interacts with its environment. The actions that the agent can perform in its environment are predefined, as is the environment itself. Given an input, the agent will perform an action, and if it is the correct action, the agent is positively reinforced. As it interacts with its environment, it learns the correct action given a specific input, maximising its performance over time. The great thing about reinforcement learning is that the training environments for these agents can be simulated, meaning training data can be created at very low cost, such as an autonomous vehicle learning how to drive in a simulated environment. Google offered a powerful example of reinforcement learning by reducing the energy consumption of its data centres by 40 per cent. The company allowed its algorithm to experiment with different data centre configurations until it learned how to optimise power consumption.

The perfect companion to your data

As we discussed in chapter 4, data has become an invaluable commodity in the digital economy, driving insight and knowledge in a way that was previously unimaginable. This has been driven in part by networks that connect devices, such as computers, mobiles or sensors, enabling the rapid transmission of data from the source to a central storage location. The technologies and protocols that form modern networks are continuously improving, meaning more data can be moved at a quicker rate. Traditionally, all this data would be stored locally in expensive data centres. Today, however, organisations have the luxury of cheaply renting storage from a public cloud provider. The cloud enables applications to be deployed globally and massive data stores to be spun up, all at the touch of a button.

Machine learning algorithms are trained by data, and this learning process requires a huge amount of computing power. Another factor that has helped make AI accessible is the drop in price of hardware — specifically, the processors and computer chips needed for this power. As the hardware improves, more complex machine learning algorithms that demand more computing power can be used, slurping up massive swaths of data on a scale that was not previously possible. This has significantly improved the accuracy with which these algorithms can make predictions, as well as opening doors to new techniques and algorithms. The end result is a virtuous cycle, in which the improvements made to the speed and capacity of computer processors have enabled new applications, begetting more demanding and effective algorithms, driving the demand for more data, which in turn requires more demand for computing power. This virtuous cycle will continue to facilitate new products, business models and strategies, which will impact all markets on a global scale.

Now cast your mind back to chapter 1, where we introduced you to the flywheel, and to chapters 4 and 5, where we showed how user data is used to improve the experience of your product or service, and platforms induce network effects by creating demand. These concepts really gain momentum when you bring machine learning into the mix. Think about a system that autonomously teaches and improves itself as more people interact with it, creating a better user experience, leading to customer lock-in because the experience outmatches anything else on the market.

There is no doubt you are already learning from your customers. However, if you can automate the process, you create an extremely scalable system that is able to learn without human intervention. And as we discussed in chapter 5, frictionless scalability is an extremely important aspect of building out your platform. The more autonomous your system is, the easier it is to get your flywheel spinning, and the faster it spins. Remember, first-mover advantage is critical, as, just like network effects, the growth associated with data network effects is exponential.

As you can see, machine learning has great potential to augment the value of your data. However, putting the right algorithm in place is a difficult task. The rest of this chapter will focus on helping you successfully implement machine learning.

Five crucial factors in applying AI successfully

Investment in artificial intelligence and machine learning technology is only going to increase. As more money is invested, the value of the resulting algorithms and the associated knowledge actually diminishes over time, as they become more abundant and less rivalrous in nature. Algorithms themselves will become less of a competitive advantage. According to entrepreneur and artificial intelligence expert Beau Cronin, the most important factors in the successful application of artificial intelligence and machine learning are data, computing power, algorithms and talent (see figure 6.1, overleaf). He argues that data is the hardest to come by, followed by talent, computing power and algorithms.

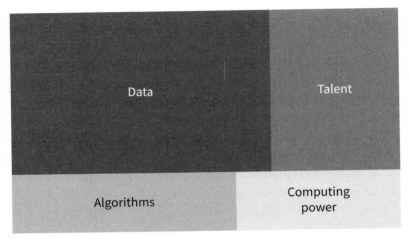

Figure 6.1: factors in the successful application of AI

With respect to data, we completely agree that this is the hardest part to come by. This is because the data sets required for machine learning need to be large and complete. Typically, pre-digital incumbents do not have these types of data sets for many of the potential use cases of machine learning because they haven't had the infrastructure in place to collect them. We also believe that data is fundamentally the most important, not only with respect to artificial intelligence and machine learning, but also to your economic engine, for without data, there can be no learning, no data network effects and no flywheel.

Many algorithms are accessible online and free, but the data has to be unique if it is to provide any sort of competitive advantage. Acquiring unique data sets that can be useful here requires a considerable amount of effort and time. This is why data is one of the three key enablers that make up the Digital Maturity Index (DMI), which we discussed at the beginning of part II. Given that we already have a chapter dedicated to data, we'll focus on the other three components here.

There is a vast array of algorithms and techniques that can be used in the application of machine learning, depending on the problem. For instance, the algorithm to determine the likelihood of something happening, such as converting a potential lead into a sale, is called a classification model, while predicting how much of something is likely — for example, the total customer spend on your ecommerce site — is called a regression model. The algorithm is the brain of artificial intelligence, and in machine learning it evolves over time as it learns from the data. Applying the right algorithm is integral to the solution's success. Applying the wrong algorithm can lead to lacklustre results and wasted money. Knowing which algorithm to apply, and applying it effectively, is a function of having talent that is knowledgeable in both artificial intelligence and your business.

Up until this point, we wholeheartedly agree with Beau. But his artificial intelligence thesis is missing a key component that is integral to the successful application of artificial intelligence, and that is the *user experience*. Artificial intelligence needs to be implemented in a systems context. Bolting on artificial intelligence for the sake of it does not provide the user with a fluid and seamless experience. In fact, it probably detracts from the experience. The application of artificial intelligence should seem natural and enhance the customer's interactions in an unobtrusive way. Currently, the application of artificial intelligence has been more technology driven than business driven, which has led to unnatural experiences — for example, online chatbots that accept only a small number of commands and spit out error messages if a user enters anything unexpected. These underwhelming results are caused by a lack of understanding on the demand side and overselling on the supply side.

Returning to this 'systems' approach, the application of AI has to be integrated so it fits snugly into the customer's lifecycle, as well as the underlying business infrastructure, processes and personnel. Machine learning can be applied to many activities in the value chain, enhancing the value of that specific activity, and thus the overall value provided to the customer. One example of machine learning is forecasting demand based on historical data, ensuring the adequate amount of stock is available in the right location to meet seasonal demand. Another common example is the implementation of automatic processes to send customers targeted advertising based on their past purchase behaviour or interaction with a retailer. In these ways, algorithms can be used to enhance customer interactions, whether that be entirely digital, a combination of machine learning and human, or further along the value chain, sitting as a layer above your data, used to unearth new patterns and drive decision making. As we discussed in chapter 3, it's all about starting small, gaining buy-in, then building out your machine learning capabilities. Over time, intelligent algorithms can become commonplace throughout your organisation, creating a system that evolves through learning, and providing your customers with ever-increasing value. We call this a system of intelligence.

Recalling chapter 1, artificial intelligence by itself will not be enough to construct a wide moat, but a system of intelligence will be. If you can create a system that integrates computing power, the right algorithms, vast and varied types of data, business talent and a great user experience, you have a very effective moat. The fuel of these systems is obviously data, but what generates the data is the day-to-day activities of your business and the interactions your customers have with you. The more customer interactions you can support, the more data you can ascertain.

This is where the power of the platform comes into play. Think of your platform as the distribution channel that creates new interactions and acts as a two-way conduit in which data can travel both up and down between parties. A system of intelligence enhances the experience of your platform, driven off the back of the data collected from your company's day-to-day activities. It can also be used to encourage more customers and more interactions. More platform usage generates more data, which your system of intelligence can use to further improve itself and the offering. The more data you produce, the smarter your product becomes. This is the data flywheel we've spoken about many times in this book, and your system of intelligence plays an important role in this virtuous improvement cycle. There will also be a large human aspect in this improvement process, which will also be driven by the data you collect, but the more automation you build into the loop, the more your flywheel will spin.

Creating a system of intelligence

So how do you go about creating and implementing a system of intelligence? The key is to keep it simple to begin with. Author and systems theorist John Gall wrote:

> A complex system that works is invariably found to have evolved from a simple system that worked. A complex system designed from scratch never works and cannot be patched up to make it work. You have to start over, beginning with a working simple system.

This is especially true in creating a system of intelligence. Trying to over-engineer from the outset is destined to fail. It's also important to start small and build momentum internally to win over key stakeholders. The creation of a system of intelligence is a highly iterative process that requires data experts and business domain experts to combine their knowledge and work together. When undertaking the task of integrating AI into your organisation, we recommend you take the following approach.

UNDERSTAND

It is critical that before you invest any money into AI, you first understand AI and its implications for your organisation and market sector. Make sure you do your research and upskill the necessary business leaders before you start consulting with vendors or hiring AI experts.

IDENTIFY

Second, identify a series of potential business-led AI projects — systems of intelligence. For each project, define the key metrics you want to improve through the application of these systems. These metrics must be easily measurable so you can continue to track the optimisation of your algorithms, as well as help define the success criteria for each project.

Look for areas where a decision needs to be made or an output produced given a specific input. Typically, these are repetitive tasks that require some form of human judgement. According to leading AI expert Andrew Ng, if it takes a human about one second to perform a mental task, it can probably be automated with AI, either now or in the future. Other opportunities lie in large data sets, as AI is fantastic at crunching through data to help make predictions and recommendations. Remember that the successful implementation of AI requires large data sets regardless of the activity, and that there are also ethical and legal considerations associated with using and storing some forms of data, such as customer data.

RANK AND PLAN

Once you have selected your projects and defined their success criteria, rank the projects based on their impact on the bottom line. When doing this, you need to consider how much it is going to cost to implement and maintain them. Conducting this research typically requires someone with

AI knowledge, so if possible hire someone with this skill set to lead the initiative. There are many ways to go about implementing AI solutions, including using vendors or open-source solutions, so make sure those leading your AI initiative evaluate all possible options before moving forward (we discuss open-source software in more detail in chapter 8). Finally, include personnel costs, as training these systems requires the help of your expert staff.

In conducting this analysis, you should have enough information to put together a series of project plans. We don't recommend executing them all at once. First choose the projects that aren't too costly but will provide good returns. If successful, these initial projects will play an important role in gaining buy-in from key stakeholders within the organisation. Consider your first project as a proof of concept.

EXECUTE AND MONITOR

Once you have selected your first project, it's time to execute. The most time-consuming aspect of implementing a system of intelligence is preparing the data. Choosing well-labelled and -structured data sets means much less preparation work is required. If your organisation is lacking in data expertise and infrastructure, you will struggle to implement any machine learning solution effectively, so ensure these foundations are in place before moving forward (see chapter 4 for more on data).

As with any software implementation, you will need to undertake rigorous testing before launching to ensure your system is producing the correct outcomes, so factor in adequate time for this. Because this is your first project, lay the foundations to building out the necessary infrastructure and skill base for all future projects.

Machine learning is a process of continuous refinement and thus not something that can be set up and left. Over time, as consumer behaviours or internal processes change, a machine learning algorithm can become less accurate. Therefore, these algorithms will need to be checked regularly to assess relevance and, if necessary, redeveloped.

There are a couple of other things you also need to consider.

Assembling your team

When it comes to choosing your team, remember that both business and technical skill sets are required. When selecting the technical members, it's imperative that they understand your business, the market in which you play and the root of the problem you are trying to solve. They must also be able to explain in lay terms what they are doing and what they have done. If they cannot articulate how this will help your bottom line or the business imperative, then you're already starting on the back foot. The question to ask here is: does the business case stack up? This is a two-way street, and it's important that you and your business team take the time and make the effort to understand at a high level how artificial intelligence and machine learning work, as well as their potential and limitations. People have varying expectations, and you need to be realistic about what AI can do to ensure the project runs as smoothly as possible.

The five Vs of big data

One of the more challenging aspects of the application of artificial intelligence is in finding the right problem to tackle. You may have a number of business processes or customer touchpoints that could be optimised, but if you don't have the data to train an algorithm in these areas, then this isn't a good place to start. Instead, focus on lower hanging fruit. We will show you how to identify a use case for machine learning and a system of intelligence. To begin, and building on what you learned in chapter 4, you need to think about the five Vs of big data for your systems of intelligence:

1. **Velocity.** This is the pace at which data flows from its sources. A system of intelligence that has a data feed closer to real time is much more responsive to changes within its environment, enabling better decision making and customer experiences.

2. **Volume.** For best results, machine learning requires large data sets. The more data you have to train your system of intelligence, the better the output.

3. **Variety.** Having a large amount of variation in your data means your system of intelligence has a wider scope or environment in which to operate. This, in turn, means it can understand more variables and consider more aspects to make better decisions.

4. **Veracity.** If your data cannot be trusted, then obviously your system's output cannot be trusted. You need to implement appropriate checks to ensure the data your system of intelligence is receiving is trustworthy.

5. **Value.** Will the intelligent algorithm you use, the data you feed it and the system of intelligence you create provide value? If so, who to? You should always be thinking about this in the application of artificial intelligence.

Now you've refreshed your sense of the role of data as fuel for your system of intelligence, you can focus on identifying a business-led use case for machine learning.

Constructing a highly defensible moat

Systems of intelligence can be used to replace or supplement expert judgement and manual decision-making processes. Predictive models are faster because automated decision making can be applied to millions of data sets simultaneously. For humans to do this work would be extremely expensive and time-consuming. These models are often more accurate than their human counterpart and don't suffer from being inconsistent. Once the model has been trained, it is cheaper to run than a human employee, especially at scale (think digital distribution).

Artificial intelligence harnesses the power of these predictive models, but, as we've mentioned before, the algorithm alone is not enough to act as your digital moat. Your moat comes from creating a system of intelligence that drives customer interactions, and creates lock-in as the experience becomes more personalised and effective. So what constitutes a real system of intelligence that creates a defensible moat? Here, in no particular order, are five different ideas.

VERTICAL EXPERTISE

In many industries, there are specific domains where human capital, business-specific knowledge and intellectual property can act as a moat. Through harnessing this expertise, you can create a system of intelligence that will provide a competitive advantage relative to a system of intelligence created by a team *without* this expertise. Note that artificial intelligence does not tell you where and how it should be applied — that is a human job. This relates back to having both the technical and business capabilities in one team, and having them work together. So where and with whom does your domain expertise lie? Can it be combined with data to create a system of intelligence?

Just a quick note. Some don't categorise focusing on one vertical as a 'system', but we certainly do. Even in one vertical there are numerous data sets from varied sources to collect, and these can be used to unlock huge amounts of value when coupled with machine learning.

PERSONALISATION AT SCALE

A system of intelligence must be scalable, in that the owner shouldn't have to make large changes whenever there is a new user. The point is to build a system that can easily bring in new users, while providing them with a personalised experience from the first interaction. The marginal cost of providing a user a personalised experience through a system of intelligence is zero as it is powdered by software. Having to create this bespoke experience manually, however, isn't a system of intelligence and is costly with respect to marginal costs. This attribute is probably more critical with customer-facing solutions, but is important for internal systems as well.

MAN AND MACHINE

In many circumstances, the best outcome will be achieved through a mix of human and machine intelligence. This is similar to the vertical expertise moat, but different in that an expert and a trained intelligent algorithm will work together to provide optimal outcomes. Your system is then half man, half machine. This has proven to work well where there is a need for human emotion, judgement or creativity. For instance, AI can help a customer service representative troubleshoot problems faced by customers and find solutions extremely quickly, while the customer service representative can convey the solution in a manner and tone that is agreeable to the customer. This combination creates highly defensible moats, as both the intelligent algorithm and the human expert evolve over time, creating a hybrid flywheel.

NETWORK INTELLIGENCE

The network effects of data partners with an algorithm to provide incremental value to players across the value chain. The more parties involved, the more data it can use to provide increased value. The flywheel kicks in, and more value attracts more parties and more interactions. Network intelligence on a platform can improve the experience on both the demand side (recommendation engines recommend products to customers based on purchasing behaviours of similar customers, as well as other data sources like weather or seasons), and the supply side (pricing optimisation engines or forecasting engines help sellers set the price of their goods and forecast demand based on data sources like time of the year, the purchasing habits of similar customers, weather, and remaining and future stock).

INTEGRATION INTELLIGENCE

When smart algorithms meet physical hardware, an almost infinite range of opportunities present themselves. Integrating hardware and software so they are built to run optimally together creates tangible products that provide new experiences and open up new business opportunities. Incredibly strong moats can be created through building products that live in both the digital and physical worlds. A prime example of this is the iPhone 8, which was built with an Apple-designed GPU (graphics processing unit), allowing Apple to optimise the machine learning workloads running on the iPhones, which is especially handy for Apple's intelligent personal assistant, Siri.

The barriers you raise will not come from intelligence alone, but from the system you create. These ideas offer five ways to think about how to create a system of intelligence. There are varying degrees of overlap between them, but they suggest a number of different ways to approach the creation of a highly defensible digital moat. Before proceeding, always ask yourself: will this improve the bottom line in a sustainable way? Whether through cost saving, creating a better customer experience that encourages more users, or helping you make faster and better decisions, all of these factors affect the bottom line. Technology for the sake of technology does not.

The power of these intelligent systems is the continual, progressive, automated learning from data. The question that then needs to be asked is: is my company's organisational design and culture ready to respond proactively to this evolving intelligence? An intelligent system continues to improve over time, and your teams need to move with it. Otherwise, the investment in machine learning is pointless. In fact, it could cost your company valuable time and resources.

If you're going to implement machine learning and create a system of intelligence, make sure your teams can respond and move with agility. Windows are small, opportunities are big, and missing out can be devastating. In the end, to utilise artificial intelligence, you need a culture that is willing to learn continuously. Therefore, the implementation of your system of intelligence should certainly be a key priority of your Engine B, which isn't shackled to your old ways of doing business. Rather, your new agile team can operate in an agile way — continuously learning, adapting and improving with the technology, which in turn is driven by the people and hardware that interact with it.

Questions

1. Fill in the blank: 'If our competitors applied artificial intelligence to _____, we'd be in serious trouble.'

2. Which key decisions or operations, if any, would you consider turning over entirely to artificial intelligence systems? Which would you do while keeping a human involved as part of the process?

(continued)

Questions (*cont'd*)

3. What new products or services could be created by combining the capabilities of artificial intelligence with a human touch (the 'hybrid')?

4. What are your most important pattern-matching, recommendation, classification and prediction activities? Are you exploring machine learning solutions for any of them?

5. If you have business processes that require a lot of person-to-person interaction, is this because your customers (or employees, suppliers or other partners) value it, or because they don't have an equally efficient digital alternative?

6. Are you tracking your decisions and the forecasts made by people and algorithms in your organisation? Do you know which ones are doing a good job?

7. Of the tasks currently being done by humans in your organisation, which will be the hardest for computers to take over? Why do you believe this?

8. Which do you think are generally more biased: algorithms or humans?

9. Looking at the existing tasks and processes in your job or organisation, what do you see as the ideal division of work between humans and machines?

Chapter summary

Bill Gates writes, 'We always overestimate the change that will occur in the next two years and underestimate the change that will occur in the next ten. Don't let yourself be lulled into inaction.' Machine learning has the market buzzing, with many businesses scrambling for anything they can get their hands on. But if you take a step back, you'll see that machine learning is more hype than quality. Don't get us wrong, the field has come a long way, and of course there have been some great successes. But you need to be wary of those who claim it is your enterprise's panacea.

That said, investments and learnings now will serve your organisation extremely well in the future. It's important to build a company that is able to work with and leverage machine learning to provide better experiences and make faster, more accurate decisions. So, when it comes to picking a use case, you need to ensure you're focusing on an area that makes a huge difference to your product or how you operate internally. Don't expect any positive results if it feels like you've just tacked artificial intelligence on. Remember, a fantastic, clean customer experience is critical to the adoption of artificial intelligence. Key to this is focusing on where your intellectual property and data — your strengths — lie, and figuring out how you can leverage these assets to build a highly defensible moat. A system of intelligence becomes truly intelligent when it is able to capture data from multiple sources and is enhanced by human intelligence. Being first to market and employing data network effects will also be critical to ensuring your flywheel spins faster than your competitors'.

Culture and organisational design will play an integral role in ensuring you are able to harness the power of your system of intelligence. You must have a culture that is willing to learn and evolve over time if your organisation is to implement machine learning, which at its core also evolves over time. If your company is static and unable to make changes on the fly, then your system of intelligence will provide no real benefit to your organisation. Remember, one of the key moats here is created when human and machine work, learn and improve together. Therefore, when it comes to organisational design, it makes sense to have these systems of intelligence as part of your Engine B, which can learn and adapt to the technology, as well as champion the application of these intelligent systems throughout the business as your Engine B builds momentum.

This brings us to the end of part II. You're now ready to proceed to part III, where you'll discover three vital accelerators of digital transformation.

Part III
Accelerating change

In this final part of the book, we provide you with solutions to accelerate change. We focus on three areas that as an agent of change and a senior leader within your business, you have the power to control and influence:

» investment management

» technology risk management

» your board and directors.

These three key areas can significantly affect the rate of your digital transformation. We have observed that these change-making areas are too often discussed as an afterthought, if at all, among executives pursuing a digital agenda. Given their critical importance to digital transformation, we deemed it necessary to spend some time exploring how these areas impact on the strategy, culture and enablers we have already covered.

Chapter 7 will examine the correlation between digital innovation, growth and investment. We will explain how accepted ROI calculations and traditional business case scenarios need to adapt for emerging technology. We will also walk through the challenges you are likely to face in securing funds to help accelerate your digital strategy, and we will provide two approaches to investment conversations that focus on longevity as well as growth.

Investments and growth strategies have inherent risk, for which you, as a leader, are accountable. For pre-digital incumbents, the likelihood and severity of technology-based risks is increasing as people move their business and social interactions online, and data is exchanged between companies. In our new economy, business leaders typically struggle to manage three domains of risk — cybersecurity, open-source software and the adoption of cloud computing. Each of these domains is unpacked in chapter 8, where we will propose solutions to ensure you can grow quickly while ensuring you manage your risks accordingly.

Finally, we have dedicated a chapter to boards and directors. The importance of the board in a digital transformation cannot be underestimated. It's therefore important that you provide your directors with a clear understanding of the challenges all companies face during a digital transformation, as well as an informed vision of the opportunities. In this chapter, we explore how you as a leader can communicate with, and secure the support of, your board as you lead your organisation to success in the digital economy.

CHAPTER 7
Investment management

It's not because things are difficult that we dare not venture.
It's because we dare not venture that they are difficult.

Seneca

According to KPMG, since 2010 there has been a steady rise in venture capital money invested globally, from US$10 billion in the first quarter of 2010 to US$39.4 billion in the third quarter of 2017 — a compound annual growth rate of 21.6 per cent. Unfortunately, this capital has made its way to anywhere but the pre-digital incumbent. No doubt you've seen how a fledgling start-up can raise $1 million in a few weeks with a glossy-looking pitch deck and a few handshakes. For a similar project to be approved within a pre-digital incumbent, it could take months of waiting for the 'right' moment in a budget cycle, numerous meetings, endless documentation and an abundance of stakeholders to manage, most of whom may not understand your proposition. In other words, it's an uphill battle to secure funds within an existing business unit.

There's no two ways about it: you need capital to execute on some or all of the recommendations set out in this book. Investments in data, platforms or systems of intelligence can be significant. Staying relevant in the face of digital disruption requires speed and agility, and without the right investment mentality and processes in place, you'll find yourself stymied as opportunity slips right past.

In this chapter, we introduce an investment management mindset designed to help you make quick and intelligent decisions when investing in your Engine B. We also explain how to manage your Engine A investments, with a heavy focus on streamlining, and optimising cost and operations. Adopting the mindset and framework outlined in this chapter will ensure your investment decisions are efficient and directly aligned to your company's overall strategy. It's time to kill decision-making paralysis before it kills you.

The three types of innovation

Before we discuss an investment mindset and framework, it's important to understand the different types of innovation. After all, innovation drives investment, and investment drives growth. Author Clayton Christensen identifies three types of innovation you can use to describe the nature of an investment. Although this theory of innovation is now 20 years old, it is becoming even more relevant as digital becomes increasingly central to your business strategy. Christensen describes the three types of innovation as:

- » disruptive innovation
- » sustaining innovation
- » efficiency-based innovation.

DISRUPTIVE INNOVATION

Disruptive innovation converts a 'high-end' product, such as a mainframe computer in the 1970s or an automobile in the 1930s, into something more affordable and accessible. It's desirable in capital-rich economies as it generates economic growth and creates job opportunities in exchange for (often risky) investments. Disruptive innovation tends to start with a poorly distributed and expensive product. Think of the supercomputer in the 1970s, a machine so unwieldy that the CEO of Digital Equipment Corporation Ken Olson infamously quipped, 'There is no reason anyone would want a computer in their home.' Over time, innovations in miniaturisation — along with the effects of Moore's Law, halving the cost of computing power every 18 months — put personal computers into everyone's hands. The outcome is Apple's 2008 iPhone, which packed as much power as a 1985 Cray-2 supercomputer. Because powerful computing products are now available to the masses rather than just a select few, they create new jobs beyond just service and support, such as app developers, and new businesses, which use the iPhone to connect with customers. This is just one example of how disruptive innovation can unlock huge amounts of value not only at the company level, but also on a global scale. For these innovations to flourish, however, they need capital.

SUSTAINING INNOVATION

In contrast to disruptive innovation, sustaining innovation is the process of fine-tuning your company's business by making a good product or service better. These types of innovations are very important for maintaining or increasing margins relative to the competition. Sustaining innovations do not create jobs, as companies fight for customers in a mature market, which in return creates little net growth. This is a result of the fact that if you buy the latest generation of a product or service, you won't then buy the previous version that isn't as good. There is no new market created.

As another example, take car manufacturers. Each year they update their range, introducing new features and benefits to address increasing competition and expectations from consumers. Or, alternatively, in the finance industry, new consumer debt products provide flexibility, ease of use, loyalty point schemes or greater affordability in an effort to gain market share and address increasing expectations. These sustaining innovations generate new products to sell, but not new buyers or new economies.

EFFICIENCY-BASED INNOVATION

Last, a speciality of Japan and China is efficiency innovation, which is doing more with less. Efficiency innovations increase free cash flow but cut jobs, often dramatically. Toyota pioneered efficiency-based innovation by continuously seeking to improve its processes. In doing so, it created just-in-time manufacturing, which is the precursor to the lean manufacturing model employed by thousands, if not millions, of companies across the world.

Before we move on, there's one more point we'd like to raise, and that's an issue with financial metrics.

Balancing short-term returns and long-term investments

No doubt you use a number of key financial metrics, typically ratios, to determine the performance of your business. The issue with a number of these metrics is that they are designed to measure short-term results, such as efficiency or how quickly you can make a return on your assets. These ratios have become the go-to source for measuring success. This is fine if you are happy working on efficiency-based innovations. But as the leader of a company undergoing digital transformation, you're no longer satisfied with incremental improvements, which means you face a dilemma.

Traditional economic principles and doctrines of finance favour investments where returns are optimised in the short term. This type of thinking has no doubt been inculcated into your company. In reality, ratios obscure the need to invest in the future. Simply doing what you've done in the past, but more efficiently, will not help you meet the needs of the digital customer. We're not saying you should completely neglect these financial metrics — just recognise they aren't the be-all and end-all.

Reflect on the suggestions early in chapter 2 that in order to focus on a healthy balance of short-term efficiencies and long-term investments you should establish both an Engine A and Engine B. Each engine is designed with a different set of objectives and performance metrics but connected through a common purpose. As part of this, consider the allocation of funds to Engine A and how that compares with Engine B. The funding mix will vary depending on the change taking place in your industry and the pace of change you feel is required to stay competitive.

The investor's mindset

The biggest investing challenges you face are resource allocation and prioritisation.

In chapter 2, you learned the benefits of having both an Engine A and an Engine B — two distinct ways in which you structure and operate your business, each with different objectives. Putting this concept in investment management terms, you need to take a venture capitalist approach to your Engine B by focusing aggressively on scale and growth, as well as taking every practical measure to make it work. At the same time, you need to take a private equity approach to your Engine A, which means creating a robust and efficient business where cash flow is king. In this section, we reveal three ways to help you develop an investor's mindset.

CREATE A CULTURE OF INNOVATION

To support these two investment styles (venture capital and private equity), company culture plays an integral role. It creates an environment in which people are willing to take calculated risks, and management isn't afraid to fail. This freedom of action is vital when taking a venture capital approach to investing, as no matter how much due diligence a company undertakes, there is always an element of risk. Without cultural reinforcement, cash flow pressure on the new-growth business and the existing business reigns supreme. If a new disruption from a competitor hits the market, things will really start to fall apart as resources, both financial and human, diminish. At this point, a company is forced to invest frantically in the vain hope of finding a new source of revenue before it's too late, as the company's old, profit-making business declines. It's a lot easier to adopt a venture capital mindset when there is money rolling in and failures can be absorbed.

MOVE FASTER

Nearly all of the financial metrics used by pre-digital incumbents rely on some measure of time. Pre-digital incumbents are also prone to over-planning and under-executing. For any new project, they fall back on their old investing methods, looking at how quickly they can make a return on investment, as well as fashioning financial models and glossy presentations to be scrutinised over in endless steering committees. All this does is waste valuable time that might better have been spent in-market, learning from customers and gaining a competitive advantage.

In many cases, the time and effort spent planning is greater than the actual project itself. Three-year strategic plans no longer work, nor do annual budget and planning cycles. How can someone plan three years ahead when technology is changing so quickly? Worse, sticking rigidly to a three-year strategic plan as the market shifts in an entirely new direction is like throwing money down the drain. As a leader, you need to emphasise the importance of getting things done and learning from mistakes along the way.

A focus on tactical execution does not mean that strategic planning is no longer valuable — it simply must be seen as a continuous process. In 2005, Steve Jobs said, 'To me, ideas are worth nothing unless executed. They are just a multiplier. Execution is worth millions.' The most valuable leaders today are those who can move fast, get things done and plan strategically, all at the same time. Your challenge is to speed up execution in your business. We've talked about the cultural drivers; now how can you enable execution from an investment standpoint? Here are five tips to help you move faster:

1. Be clear on the financial metrics you expect for each type of investment to avoid teams wasting time developing investment cases that will never hit the mark.

2. Set and communicate realistic expectations in terms of investment decision-making cycles.

3. Limit, and be clear on, who needs to be involved in an investment decision to avoid stakeholder management that's disproportionate to the level of investment sought.

4. Discourage plans where precision is prioritised over accuracy. Too often plans are produced with numerous, interrelated assumptions that complicate and obscure the two or three key assumptions that need to be proved in order for an investment to be successful.

5. Identify a small number of points of strategic alignment that are non-negotiable, rather than trying to do everything in one project. For example, your investment objective might target a select demographic of your market, a characteristic of a competitor's product or service, or the profile of an untapped target buyer. This uncompromising prioritisation will help ensure your investment decisions tie back to your overarching strategy for success.

ENCOURAGE INVESTMENT EFFICIENCY

Start-ups move fast and get things done because they reward and promote managers who are highly efficient and focus on execution, rather than just talking about it. But these types of managers aren't just in start-ups. They are in every organisation; you just need to give them the space and tools to execute. When looking for leaders in your company, our experience indicates there is a particular commercially oriented mindset that will optimise your return on investment, regardless of whether you are operating in Engine A or Engine B. That mindset can be summed up by three distinct attributes:

1. They understand the cost of regret

As strange as this concept might sound, regret has a tangible cost. It is incurred when a project needs reworking or is a failure. Regret is the human response to making the wrong decision. The cost of regret can lead decision makers to spend long periods of time collecting information to make a perfect decision, and can paralyse managers from making any decision at all. Regret aversion has a particular bearing on digital transformation because many pre-digital businesses know it as a hangover from the era of traditional IT projects. There was a time when implementing technology always meant big, expensive and untested, so leaders spent years planning and building project roadmaps in an attempt to ensure success. Now, thanks to capabilities like cloud computing, companies can deliver much smaller 'pieces of value' for a nominal cost.

As a leader, you have a role in communicating the new truth that a single project failure no longer destroys the bottom line, and can be fixed and improved upon quickly. This will minimise the regret incurred and free your best managers to act, rather than over-engineer a solution. The cloud removes the need for costly on-premise infrastructure, and allows organisations to build and deploy solutions from anywhere in the world. It has also led to the creation of new delivery approaches that allow for rapid development times and shorter customer feedback loops, enabling a more iterative approach. Managers who understand that the cost of regret varies depending on the size and flexibility of the project will spend the appropriate amount of time collecting the minimum necessary information to make a decision, so they can spend more time on execution.

2. They focus on burn rate

Burn rate refers to the rate at which a new company spends its initial capital. But the concept has broader uses as well. Every time your teams run a meeting, for example, have your managers considered how much it costs? They could calculate the cost using this formula:

$$\text{Combined salaries (as hourly rate)}$$
$$\text{of participants} \times \text{meeting length} = \text{cost of meeting}$$

Have you calculated the cost of your team for a day? Thinking about projects in terms of burn rate often changes your mindset around how you make decisions and what is actually important. A project is just a controlled burn of money. It's important to remember that the money is limited, but the results aren't. Great managers can control this burn, get the maximum output and deliver higher quality. Here are a few tips on how they can do this:

» **Measure at all times.** Acknowledge the cost of time in absolute and opportunity cost terms. This will help you recalibrate decisions more regularly.

» **Less is more.** Managing large, expensive teams is difficult and adds unnecessary pressure in terms of the related burn rate.

» **Do not conflate hourly rates and output.** They are not the same thing.

3. They actively assess value

Businesses often get caught up in the projects of consulting engagements, architecture assignments and planning. These initiatives can deliver well-researched information and recommendations to the buyer of the services. Too often, however, the resulting reports are not distributed widely or contain recommendations that require a different level of executive stakeholder buy-in to implement. The reports can also be costly. Has the business realised the value of that investment? Investment-oriented leaders think differently, repeatedly questioning and assessing where the value lies. This continuous process needs to be applied to everything, from projects to personnel. This approach has less of a temporal element than return on investments, allowing the manager to focus on quality outputs, rather than just wins.

Questions

1. In your business, does innovation drive investment and, in turn, growth?

2. If you could lower the cost of regret, how would this speed things up in your business?

3. Imagine a screen in your office showing the daily burn rate for your team. How could that change the way you do things and the decisions you make?

4. Have you measured the amount of investment going to sustaining, efficiency-based or disruptive innovation initiatives?

5. How many of your investments are focused on in-year or short-term returns, and how does this align with your strategy?

6. To what extent would your leadership team change their focus if they were comfortable with the three types of innovation?

7. Relative to your peers and emerging competitors, how fast do you move and does your business change?

8. Do you have a culture, and financial performance appraisal system that supports experimentation?

Chapter summary

To apply the concepts and practical advice in this book, you must invest. This is challenging for any pre-digital incumbent organisation. Changing your approach is where the rubber hits the road and will test whether your business is serious about digital. Get this part right and everything else will fall into place. Do it badly and you will be dancing around the edges while time runs away from you.

Remember, innovation drives investment, and investment drives growth. So you need a solid understanding of innovation itself — what it is, and what it sets out to achieve strategically. Clayton Christensen's innovation theory identifies three types of innovation — efficiency-based, sustaining and disruptive. We recommend these as guiding principles for your investment strategy.

As a leader with financial responsibility, you need to develop an investor's mindset to help manage innovation and your strategies for success, and the Engine A and Engine B organisational design concepts. We have covered three approaches to investment that will accelerate change for your business:

1. Develop a venture-capital and private-equity mindset, and apply these to the Engine A and Engine B teams respectively, by creating a culture of innovation within your company.

2. Focus on the value of time, appreciating that the best way to manage risk is with a product in the market. From an investment standpoint, do everything to achieve this goal as quickly as possible.

3. Seek out and reward leaders who deliver investment efficiency. Now more than ever, leaders with a passion for efficiency will deliver results in our new digital economy. There are three attributes to look for:

   » They understand the cost of regret and execute in spite of it.

   » They continuously think about and prioritise burn rate.

   » They actively assess value without compromise in everything they do.

In the next chapter, we reveal the major trends that will keep your technology risk low, and how to manage them.

CHAPTER 8
Technology risk management

Take calculated risks. That is quite different from being rash.
George S. Patton

Technology risk management today is very different from what it was ten, or even five, years ago. In our hyper-connected world, the inherent cyber threats of doing business have increased, requiring new risk management practices to protect your company. Risk, security and legal professionals are struggling to keep up as businesses suddenly find themselves dealing with a fundamental shift in their value chains, requiring new strategies and business models to stay competitive. This may sound scary, but you have to remember that the cyber threat pales in comparison with the risk of doing nothing and choosing to ignore the need to embrace digital.

As discussed in part II, data underpins the future growth of your business, which means your organisation must develop a strong understanding of data regulation, specifically that relating to confidentiality and privacy. Legislation surrounding data is constantly changing and can be a minefield, so it's important your organisation continuously updates policies accordingly and employs or engages expertise in this area. Ensuring growth also requires a fundamental shift in how you approach technology licensing. Perpetual, one-off licences are now an outdated practice; subscriptions, or pay-as-you-go solutions, are the new norm. At the core of this change is the increasing demand for cloud services. Gartner projects a rise in global cloud computing spend from US$67 billion in 2015 to US$162 billion in 2020 — a compound annual growth rate of 19 per cent. Amazon, Microsoft, Google and many others are riding this wave, providing organisations with the opportunity to move from costly, self-managed data centre facilities to cloud-based solutions that treat computing power as a utility.

But the move to the cloud does not come without challenges. In a 2016 research report, Cybersecurity Ventures predicted cybercrime will cost the world US$6 trillion annually by 2021, up from US$3 trillion in 2015, and will be 'more profitable than the global trade of all major illegal drugs combined'. Given the statistics, it's not surprising that cybersecurity is a hot topic in the boardroom. However, moving to the cloud does not make you more susceptible to cyberattacks. In fact, if executed properly, quite the opposite is true.

Another trend over recent years has been the explosion in the use of open-source software. (Software is open source when its code is freely available, and can be modified and distributed by anyone.) Open-source software plays an important role in many software projects, because it allows organisations to repurpose software that solves someone else's problems and adapt it to solve their own problems. For lawyers and risk professionals this can be a headache, because the licensing considerations are immense and the technology nuance and understanding that's required is often outside the training or experience of non-specialists.

How, then, can you approach technology risk management — specifically the key areas of regulatory compliance, cyber-security, cloud computing and open-source software? In this chapter, we outline topics you should add to your risk agenda. And, as risk management must evolve in line with changing markets and regulations, we advocate an ongoing process for updating technology risk management to protect your brand, public trust and reputation as you grow and innovate.

Navigating the new rules of cybersecurity

With more platforms connecting machines and people than ever before, the risk of security breaches has never been higher. The simple fact is that the greater the number of people connecting with your business and sharing their data, the higher the risk. As we explored in chapters 5 and 6, platforms and systems of intelligence are complex in their engineering. As this complexity increases, so too does the cybersecurity risk.

A joint report conducted by IBM and the Ponemon Institute found that 25 per cent of data breaches were caused by a system glitch, 28 per cent by human error, and 48 per cent by malicious or criminal attacks. Vulnerabilities are inevitable, but putting the right processes in place can dramatically reduce cybersecurity risk. Here, we outline five ways to do that.

ENSURE CONTROL AND CONSISTENCY OF CUSTOMER DATA

If data about your customers is lost or stolen, the resulting reputational damage and cost can cripple your business. Industry reports estimate that over 30 per cent of customers discontinue their relationship with a company after a data breach. For this reason, you should be clear about the way you manage all customer-related data. Having this data scattered across numerous applications can lead to you simply losing track of where it is all stored, and inevitably there will be different standards applied to its safekeeping across the different data stores. Therefore, you need to put sensitive customer data in one system or database, ensuring you then have a consistent approach to managing it. Having all your data in one spot makes it much easier to protect, as you can enforce common standards and practices. You should also consider the way in which sensitive data is managed, whether it is 'at rest' (data that's been written and is not being accessed or transmitted) or 'in motion' (data that is in the process of being transferred via the internet or a network between separate storage locations).

REFRESH INTERNAL CONTROLS AND POLICIES

Most companies have spent decades implementing control frameworks in an effort to safeguard their internal IT functions. Annual audit and testing processes provide assurance about server security, permissions, access points and the like. However, when you amplify your efforts to connect with customers online, your risk profile changes. As you collect more customer data, you create more opportunities for cyberattacks. This risk is compounded by the bring-your-own-device-to-work movement that many companies are adopting. Refresh your policies and controls to deal with these situations, and increase the frequency of review and assurance activities. There are advisers you can contact and frameworks you can adopt to ensure you have the basics covered for your industry standard. Consider, however, whether the bar you or they set is high enough for your business objectives and values. Don't hold back on enlisting specialists to challenge the concept of 'best practice'.

TRUST AND RESPECT THE CLOUD

There is a common presupposition that the cloud is riskier than using on-premise servers. This is not true. At every level, there is no comparison between the security of the cloud and that of your own data centre. The ongoing proliferation of cloud incentivises companies to prevent even the most sophisticated hacks and viruses. Trusted cybersecurity brands are actively increasing the sophistication of their threat detection, decryption, and virus or malware removal tools to provide robust protection specific to the cloud, whereas data centre security innovations are not advancing at the same rapid pace.

As a further benefit to your business, the cloud makes it extremely easy to access and launch global software solutions, including security programs, and it's all done with the click of a button. This agility puts greater emphasis on the design and configuration of systems within the cloud, whereas your on-premise solutions have to be customised and upgraded independently. Cloud vendors offer a wide range of services and tools, and release new ones every week, so having a process in place to ensure the appropriate vetting and configuration of services is vital. Here are some pragmatic ways to achieve this:

» As you would in the development of software, develop a roadmap of the services you plan to adopt from cloud vendors and communicate this to your team.

» Regularly — say, once a quarter — step back, and understand what's available and how this could be applied to the solutions you are working on.

» Ensure you have a strategy to allow innovation and experimentation without constraints. Look to employ what is called a 'sandbox environment' to test and trial new ideas and initiatives in a simulated environment before going live. For live systems, use a 'locked down' environment where your security and risk management controls are well defined.

SOFTWARE ENGINEERING QUALITY IS CRITICAL

Throughout this book, we have emphasised the importance of responding to the pace of change. Do not make haste by compromising on software engineering quality. Neglecting quality could be the end of your business, as you will burn through unnecessary time managing software development risks, including security, performance, scale or misalignment with your strategy. Software engineering quality can be difficult to define, and is not as simple as determining whether or not the software 'works'. To determine if quality is at the right level, engage with your software engineers and other managers to understand the effectiveness of updating or implementing new software in your business. If most of the answers to the following questions are 'yes', you likely have a problem. You should then enlist experts to help you work through these challenges.

» Do your managers report that systems and programs seem harder and more complex than they were before a major software update or new implementation occurred?

» Does your team fix a bug only to find it reappears in a week or so?

» Do users report that the performance of software is variable across the application?

» Do testing efforts seem exhausting, and increasingly complex, even when they relate to minor changes?

» Do the cost or time estimates associated with changes seem disproportionate to the intuitive level of effort involved?

» Is your software development team's velocity decreasing? When you were building the first version of your product, you could develop a new feature quickly, and your team used to build lots of them every iteration. Is their output slower now?

» How is morale? Is your engineering team easily demotivated by complexity or change?

There's a big difference between software development and software engineering. The difference relates largely to skill, but generally speaking, software developers focus on writing code with specific functional outcomes in mind, whereas software engineers take a more holistic, logical approach to solving complex problems in the context of scale and adaptability. Don't skimp on the right level of experience, and invest in working with engineers when you have more complex problems that need to perform and scale.

PEOPLE ARE YOUR GREATEST RISK

Software and data are ultimately controlled or accessed by people. It's not just the underworld hackers that you need to be worried about. Keep in mind the risk associated with your staff, including both honest mistakes and deliberately disruptive actions. Having adequate controls in place is vital, but the challenge is to ensure people adhere to them. It's also important that these controls don't slow the pace of day-to-day operations with unnecessary protocols. For example, limiting access to sensitive customer-related data in order to maintain data integrity and security will impede productivity. You can help reduce the risk of people compromising data security — deliberately or unwittingly — through training programs and selective audits.

As interactions with your clients move online, the trust associated with your brand is constantly at risk of cybersecurity attack. As a pre-digital incumbent, your reference point has been your on-premise IT systems, where most of your risk has been managed through a series of well-defined, relatively durable controls, with these systems being updated only occasionally to cover most risks. However, as the time between development cycles decreases and the pace of these cycles increases, redesigning your technology risk controls will be integral to ensuring you can keep up with the speed of the market while safeguarding your business from potential threats.

Open-source software may be your friend

Open source is not the bogeyman the software billionaires would like us to believe. It is software designed to be shared and, as such, is managed by an online community, typically of volunteer software engineers, that facilitates sharing and collective improvement. In fact, open source is now so pervasive in software that it is almost impossible to avoid, but it nevertheless remains a hot topic for lawyers and risk professionals. From a strategic standpoint, you must consider the opportunities that open-source software provides — 'pre-baked' solutions that you can adapt to your requirements.

Businesses around the world are using open-source software to reduce costs, apply focus to innovation efforts, and solve problems that it would be impossible or unprofitable for one company to tackle alone. Detection of phishing attacks, analysing genomes and geospatial mapping are just a few of the open-source projects underway to improve corporate and public services.

Open-source software can also be used to build new business models and create digital moats, which may sound counterintuitive to those who are used to the world of patents. In 2017, computer chip maker Nvidia decided to make the designs of one of its chips publicly available using a licensing agreement to support sharing, even though it used the same designs in some of the chips it was selling. The company's need for scale and distribution, however, was more valuable than a patent for a deep-learning chip. Nvidia decided the patent was not a significant competitive advantage. Having its technology embedded into hardware devices and integrated with third-party software solutions around the world was, in contrast, a *massive* competitive advantage. For Nvidia, making its design open source means that a host of companies are now building out an entire ecosystem around its technology. In other words, Nvidia has created a platform.

While there are many open-source licensing agreements to take into account (around 2500, in fact), don't be deterred by this. There is only one key point to understand: though open-source software is free to use, it is not free from legal obligations. Depending on the maturity of the open-source project and the size of the community supporting it, it can sometimes be unreliable and could potentially pose a security risk given its open nature. Proper due diligence must be conducted, though large open-source projects are typically well designed, documented and reviewed.

Consider the following six points if you want to properly manage and unlock the benefits of open-source software:

1. Put in place an open-source management policy that dictates which types of open-source licences are acceptable and not acceptable for your organisation. This is a specialised area and largely the realm of lawyers and risk professionals.

2. Think about the use of open-source software from a security standpoint, taking into account the inherent benefits of crowdsourced improvement, but also the drawbacks in the public and open nature of the code.

3. Ensure you have an effective code approval process so staff who may not appreciate the risks can still access the benefits of open-source software.

4. Define and implement a policy for open-source software updates. This will provide guidance to your software development teams on what to update, when and why.

5. Consider that the solution you wish to build may not be the first of its kind, and that an open-source solution very likely already exists or can be modified to meet your needs. Sites like GitHub, as largely open-source code repositories, are useful references to determine whether a solution already exists.

6. Consider open-source based business models like Nvidia, but ensure you have the in-house capabilities to support such business models, both technically and legally. Early engagement with risk and legal professionals will help in defining the process you should follow.

Open source unlocks a wealth of possibilities. Like the platform concept, it allows collaboration and openness, which can accelerate business and customer value. As with anything in the digital realm, it comes with risk that you can overcome and should not see as a deterrent. If you address the six points we've just outlined, you can mitigate most of the associated risk.

Busting the myths of cloud computing

Several years ago, the hype around cloud computing was very much just that — hype! Few cloud vendors were able to provide the level of service they advertised. Today this is no longer the case. The benefits you can realise from the cloud are so significant that there is now no excuse not to move your workloads onto the cloud. Gartner predicts that by 2020, 'a corporate "no-cloud" policy will be as rare as a "no-internet" policy is today'. In fact, Gartner expects that by 2020, more computing power will be sold by cloud providers than is sold and deployed into enterprise data centres.

The cloud brings to the table an extremely cost-effective way to develop and launch software solutions. One of the primary advantages of the cloud is elasticity. When buying on-premise solutions, typically you would purchase a server that could handle peak workloads, plus some additional buffer just to be on the safe side. This meant that for much of the year, these servers were operating well below maximum capacity. As your business grew, you would eventually have to replace these servers with bigger ones, but again you would have to think long term, purchasing servers that could handle future peak workloads. As you can appreciate, if your business is growing quickly, or if you have demanding, cyclical workloads, on-premise can become very costly. The cloud eradicates this problem as you only ever pay for what you use, meaning there is no excess capacity sitting idle. Other advantages of the cloud include global reach, reduced complexity with respect to system management and maintenance, and rapid implementation cycles.

Of course there will be challenges, but don't use them as an excuse for staying away from the cloud. Armed with an understanding of potential problems, you are in a good position to lead the charge. Here, we bust five common myths about cloud computing.

SOME APPLICATIONS DON'T RUN ON THE CLOUD

There are still some, though not many, who say you can't reconfigure an on-premise solution to work effectively in the cloud and, as a result, removing your dependence on physical infrastructure results in complexity and duplicated costs. This is simply not true. It is unsubstantiated, old-school IT thinking. If you hear this rebuttal, ask at a technical level what the limitation is and seek a second opinion from an advisory firm, because given the suite of solutions cloud vendors provide, almost anything is possible.

THE LEGAL AND RISK HURDLES ARE TOO HIGH

The best way to tackle this argument is to contrast the legalities and risks of moving to the cloud against where you are today. Consider the rights and obligations you have (or don't have) in place with your current providers, and compare these with the terms of an agreement with a cloud services leader like Google, Microsoft or Amazon. You will see by comparison that cloud vendors take away the complexity of managing physical infrastructure, offer highly competitive SLAs (service-level agreements) that meet most business requirements and provide best-in-class security, which is almost impossible for an individual enterprise to replicate. In fact, in most cases, you'd be doing yourself a disservice by not moving the majority of your IT systems to the cloud.

IT WILL COST MORE

Take another look at your total cost of ownership equation, factoring in forward replacement cycles and, more importantly, the opportunity cost associated with maintaining complex infrastructure. Sure, there may be a substantial outlay upfront when moving to the cloud. But by focusing too much on the immediate pennies, you might be missing out on huge savings down the road.

WE ALREADY HAVE OUR OWN PRIVATE CLOUD

While having your own private cloud is not a bad argument, and having your own private cloud can feel like a good position to be in, there are some issues to consider:

> » You still need to manage the underlying infrastructure and equipment.

» Nothing is really shared, so you cannot utilise the economies of scale leveraged by the large cloud providers, which lead to lower costs, faster innovation cycles and better overall solutions.

» You have no SLA in terms of availability or any other outcome; performance is managed in-house.

» You likely have a lower security profile and fewer audit accreditations compared with a cloud vendor.

» You still need to worry about it — day in, day out.

IT'S ONLY FOR DEVELOPMENT, TESTING AND NEW PROJECTS

Yes, the cloud is great for developing and testing new initiatives, but limiting the cloud to forward-looking projects suggests the infrastructure you have in place today is better than anything else on the market, which is simply not the case. Moving workloads to the cloud allows your IT team to spend less time 'keeping the lights on', and more time focusing on innovation and digital pursuits. Why anchor your IT team to managing physical infrastructure when they could be focused on unlocking new revenue streams?

Cloud computing is here, whether or not you are yet comfortable with it. The cloud provides unequivocal advantages, and the arguments against it no longer hold up. If you have not already, it is imperative that you put an effective cloud policy in place and begin to migrate your IT systems as soon as possible. Unlocking the benefits of the cloud is integral to providing a better experience for your customers and driving efficiencies internally. That said, cloud computing is not a competitive advantage — it is a basic delivery model. If you take too long to transition across, you'll be stuck playing catch-up with your competitors.

Questions

1. What policies do you have in place to protect your customer data? When were they last updated?

2. If data about your customers were to be lost or stolen, what would be the economic impact?

3. What quality assurance practices do you have in place for building software? When were they last updated?

4. Do you have a policy for managing open-source software?

5. To what extent do you use open-source software to help accelerate growth and lower costs?

6. Have you objectively weighed the positives and negatives associated with managing on-premise infrastructure compared with those related to using the cloud? Have you considered these over a medium- and long-term horizon?

7. How often does your executive team and board meet to discuss and understand technology-related risk in your business?

8. Are your employees aware of the technology-risk policies and practices you employ? How do you plan on rolling out updates and new policies?

Chapter summary

Managing technology risk is important, as the new economy changes how organisations, customers and machines interact with one another. Cloud computing, open-source frameworks and data play important roles in supporting growth in the changing ecosystem. You need technology risk practices to tap into these opportunities while mitigating cybersecurity threats.

What's most important is your control and management of customer data. In our new economy, this requires a multi-faceted approach that takes into account robust policies and control and takes a fresh look at trust. Trust will play an integral role in the success of your digital transformation. Not only will you have to trust your engineers, but you will also have to trust cloud vendors and open-source projects to help you build and operate your key systems. To be successful, organisations can no longer act as islands — working with third parties will augment your strengths.

Potential threats must not deter you. Put in place sound policies, processes and tools to protect your organisation, while ensuring you don't stifle innovation with an overly rigid framework. Protecting your customer data and your IP is critical, and absolutely achievable with well-advised protocols and practices that are continuously updated. Being digital is about removing unnecessary hurdles that curb the speed at which you operate and innovate, so don't paralyse your organisation with endless risk processes and policies — keep them lean and targeted.

In the next chapter, we shift our focus from technology risk management to your board and directors — the final piece of the puzzle.

CHAPTER 9
Advice for boards and directors

What you leave behind is not what is engraved in stone monuments, but what is woven into the lives of others.
Pericles

The bulk of this book has focused on the leaders of the pre-digital incumbent. Now we must address the resulting recommendations for boards and directors who will oversee your company's digital transformation from a strategic level. Without board-level support, the digital agenda won't take priority, and could even fall by the wayside entirely. To guide the change, directors need to understand the implications of digital for their organisation, and begin to share this with the executive team and the wider organisation.

The board plays a pivotal role: to help your company get ahead of digital disruption — not just anticipate it, but lead it and help accelerate change — and remain competitive. This chapter will provide you with solutions to ensure your board is engaged to accelerate change. We'll show you how to secure the support of your board, appoint digital experts, encourage diversity and fresh thinking, and address technology risk management at board level.

Secure support from the board

Board members must embrace the digital transformation of their business. This requires education complemented by hard facts. The truth is that the status quo must be challenged. With that in mind, here are three steps you need to take to secure the board's support for a digital transformation.

MAKE YOUR CASE

The chairman should allocate time in a board meeting for discussion on the market forces at play, and how the business could decline if everything remains the same. The objective is to create a shared sense of urgency which may be reinforced by people from other industries, venture capitalists, academics, thought leaders or consultants.

It's imperative to galvanise the board into action by ensuring they understand what is required to meet the challenges of the new economy. If they're resorting to old tricks that served them well in the pre-digital era, such as restructuring, then they will struggle to guide the business through a digital transformation. There needs to be a mutual understanding that the board may lack some skills and knowledge, which may require both education and, potentially, the addition of a digitally savvy non-executive director.

RE-EXAMINE THE BIG DECISIONS

The chair of the board is the ultimate owner of the organisation's strategy. The new rules of business and strategy set out in chapter 1 need to be worked through with the CEO.

Success in our new economy is not just about a future-ready strategy, but also about operating at speed. Directors should challenge the status quo to ensure the CEO and executive team have explored opportunities to accelerate change using the principles set out in chapter 2. Otherwise, they risk focusing solely on the core business, which is very easy to do. Without a forceful push from the board to seek out new forms of growth, your company is akin to a single-engine plane running low on fuel — highly risky and very slow.

For a business to truly succeed in the digital economy, the culture, energy, pace and people must be fit for the journey. New ideas require the freedom to test and fail, and a highly digital board understands this. A board must allow for missteps at the executive level, embrace the learnings and provide counsel where possible. This will help a culture of continuous discovery to permeate all the way through your organisation, as discussed in chapter 3.

CREATE BALANCE BETWEEN THE BOARD AND CEO

Typically, boards are accustomed to being presented to by the CEO as if they were being sold a product. Rather than doing this, they should sit down together and talk through new ideas that haven't yet been fully developed. Leverage the experience of everyone around the table in an open and candid discussion. This will encourage creativity within the group and an environment in which people are more open with one another, which in turn will spark great ideas.

The relationship and dynamic between the board and the CEO plays a critical role in the successful transformation of a company. A bad connection causes friction and slows the decision-making process. Regardless of whether there is disagreement, there must be mutual respect. For the board, there is a fine line between being too involved and not involved enough. When the pressure rises, as it inevitably will during any sort of digital transformation, board members may become uneasy with the plan, or with the CEO. A board that is constantly meddling doesn't allow the CEO to deliver a clear message and enact change. On the other hand, a board that doesn't intervene enough may not provide the necessary guidance or extra sets of eyes required to navigate the digital transformation. Every company sits somewhere on this spectrum, and there's always a sweet spot between the two extremes.

Ultimately, both board and CEO should agree that changes need to be made, and that they're in partnership to facilitate the transition — together. The board must work with the CEO and his or her team to ensure the plan is being appropriately executed, and to help resolve any unforeseen issues. On the other side of the equation, the board needs to have faith in the CEO, the management team and the plan. The CEO needs the freedom to make decisions quickly to ensure speed. It's imperative that the board doesn't suddenly push the panic button when short-term results are affected as the company looks to invest in the future, as discussed in chapter 7.

Appoint digital experts

There's no doubt that many pre-digital incumbents are pushing hard to transform their businesses. But research suggests most pre-digital incumbent leaders don't have the necessary experience to lead their companies' digital transformations. For example, according to the Korn Ferry Institute, just 1.7 per cent of non-executive directors (NEDs) on the Financial Times Stock Exchange 100 Index would qualify as 'digital' — that is, executives who have spent the bulk of their careers working for big tech or in strategic roles focused on applying the technologies described in part II of this book.

In January 2017, Calastone investigated the composition of executive leadership at ASX 100 companies, and found that 'only 40 percent of S&P/ASX 100 companies have a technologist in their leadership team'. It's fair to say that most boards of large companies would not describe themselves as digitally fluent.

The experience needed in the boardroom comes in all shapes and sizes. So what does a digitally savvy director look like? The digital director should meet the following four criteria:

1. **Experience.** The digital director should have experience in a significant operating role in a digitally born function or company, with a core focus on the technologies and digital enablers defined in chapters 4 to 6.

2. **Exposure.** The digital director should work with boards, either as a director or by regularly presenting to them.

3. **Perspective.** The digital director should have a perspective that is well-rounded and strategic. Technology expertise must be complemented with strong business and strategic acumen appropriate for board-level decisions.

4. **Currency.** The digital director should be confident with the issues, emerging trends, technologies and opportunities in the market as well as how they can be applied to the businesses successfully.

These criteria are helpful in identifying a digitally savvy director. However, you should also consider the style of the individual, depending on the digital maturity of your business and the challenges you face. An article in the *Harvard Business Review* identifies four types of digital leaders you need:

1. **Digital thinker.** This person has had little direct experience managing or working on a digital initiative, but understands at a high level what it means to be digital. This individual may have consulted or advised a digital business, but they were not born digital.

2. **Digital disruptor.** This person has deep expertise in all things digital, which often comes from experience in working for a big tech company or digitally-native business. This type of leader is likely to have less management expertise.

3. **Digital leader.** This leader has had experience within a pre-digital incumbent that has embraced digital at a strategic and operational level. This individual is likely to have had greater exposure to digital and disruptive innovation as a leader.

4. **Digital transformer.** This person has had a leadership role as part of the transformation of a pre-digital incumbent business. He or she may not be as senior as a digital leader, but they are likely to be more digitally savvy and experienced.

It can be difficult to find board members who have up-to-date technical knowledge and big company experience. Boards should therefore not limit themselves to one digitally savvy director, but seek directors across a combination of the above styles and mindsets. A variety of digital expertise will make increasingly good sense as the Fourth Industrial Revolution takes hold.

Encourage diversity and fresh thinking

Choosing leaders who faithfully abide by the will of the board only produces more of the same. Empowered leaders, who question the norm and challenge the board, bring with them a new energy to unwind outdated habits and reset the playbook for your organisation. For this to happen as part of a digital transformation, the board needs to be especially open to cutting-edge ideas and fresh thinking. This is likely to pull the board out of its comfort zone — and that's a good thing, because if change doesn't feel uncomfortable, then you're not changing much. We should point out that we aren't encouraging you to instate leaders who are likely to disagree with everything the board says.

Gender and ethnic diversity in the boardroom are significant issues. However, far fewer policies address the underlying need for diversity in expertise and thinking. Accountants, lawyers and management consultants have traditionally dominated the ranks of board directors, but in today's digital and disruptive age, the inclusion of digital leaders is imperative. Don't just choose any old self-proclaimed digital expert; seek those who can truly help your organisation thrive in the digital arena. Leaders who are efficient, yet ensure quality in their execution, are the ones who will succeed in the new economy.

Age diversity is another important consideration. Board positions have traditionally been held by those who are quite senior. But the question now is: In what ways do your board members reflect your company's target market? And are there opportunities for your board to engage with your target market in different ways? According to the US Census Bureau, the Millennial generation is currently the largest in the United States, and will be until around 2040 (when Generation Z takes the top spot). There is no hiding from the fact that if these digital-savvy Millennials aren't your biggest customer base now, they soon will be. Furthermore, not only are you selling to this demographic, but you are also employing them. This doesn't mean you need to stuff your board with Millennials. However, bringing some younger minds with a lot of potential into the mix can be an extremely successful strategy to help you relate to the people you sell to and the people you hire.

Address technology risk management at board level

In chapter 8, we covered the importance of safeguarding your new business models against technology-based risk. You'll recall we identified three topics that must be considered and focused on: cybersecurity, open-source software and cloud computing.

Before software, cloud computing and digital distribution, the focus of cybersecurity was on the hardware of the enterprise — its networks, firewalls and physical location. In our new economy, the greatest risk relates to controlling and protecting your data and software. As you know, risk management must focus primarily on how you are protecting your customer data, especially as data breaches become more common and regulation around customer data becomes more stringent. While we discussed this at length in chapter 8, there are some additional actions you can take at board level.

The board should ask the following seven questions:

1. Do our policies and control frameworks align with our current and future business model?

2. How do we protect sensitive customer data?

3. Do we have information to assess the quality or vulnerability of the software we use or develop?

4. Do we have cyber insurance?

5. Do we have a strategy for dealing with a crisis?

6. Do we have the information we need to oversee cybersecurity risks?

7. How do we protect sensitive information handled, stored and transmitted by third-party vendors?

CREATE A TECHNOLOGY ADVISORY BOARD

Setting up a technology advisory board or panel is an effective way to gain insight from individuals with a wide range of relevant technology and digital expertise. The technology advisory board should provide guidance on digital matters, such as the strategic implementation of new and emerging technologies, along with matters such as cybersecurity.

An advisory board can provide guidance to both the board of directors and the executive team, or can work closely with one of the two. If the advisory board interacts more with management, then the board of directors should confirm that the advisory board's charter and member composition adequately address the full range of technology governance and risk management issues required for the business.

APPOINT A DIGITAL EXECUTIVE TO THE AUDIT OR RISK COMMITTEE

As technology becomes more pervasive in your organisation, the ability of the audit committee, who will typically oversee risk management, to address the risk is as critical as its ability to evaluate financial risk. Working with risk teams that don't understand digital can be slow and laborious, as they approach projects and decisions using outdated processes and frameworks. Explicitly adding technology risk to the audit committee agenda — and making sure there is at least one digitally savvy executive on the committee — is highly recommended, especially where technology risk is not acute.

Questions

1. Do you consider your board to be highly digital, partially digital or non-digital, and what risk does that present for your ability to change?

2. How many of your directors would you consider digital directors and which characteristics of the digital director do you find hardest to assimilate?

3. Do members on the board truly understand the disruptive forces faced by your company? How do they communicate this knowledge?

4. Does the company have a comprehensive digital strategy (one that focuses on data, platforms and systems of intelligence), a dedicated team, leadership buy-in and appropriate funding?

5. Is the company's leadership team adequately challenged by the board, while also mentored on the risks and opportunities associated with the digital age?

6. Is technology investment owned by a specific director?

7. How digitally experienced are those responsible for your strategy? Were they 'born digital'?

8. What kind of message are you sending to the management team and the company? Is it one that promotes a sense of discovery and experimentation, focusing on bolstering your Engine A and unlocking your Engine B?

9. Are the conversations and meetings you have with the CEO about technology open and candid, with ideas flowing and people contributing and collaborating, or are they formal presentations?

Chapter summary

Boards play a critical role in the successful digital transformation of the pre-digital incumbent and in ensuring survival through the dynamic forces of the new economy. Any fundamental change to strategy requires strong leadership, and the scale of the shift we are describing absolutely has to be supported and guided by the board. As with all enterprise-wide changes, change has to be pushed from the top down, for without a driving force that has the power to enact change, the company will remain 'as is'. To drive this change, directors must possess the necessary knowledge and expertise to provide this support and guidance. The appointment of a digital director is therefore critical to helping guide the board on digital matters.

That said, digital directors cannot be the only ones leading the digital transformation agenda. While the appointment of new board members should centre on the 'digital transformer', at nearly three decades into the internet revolution, board members and executives must also understand, if not excel, in digital. As the line between online and offline becomes ever more blurred, and with every company becoming a technology company, directors need to ensure they have the skills and knowledge to lead in the new digital economy.

Some may argue that technology moves too quickly to keep up with, and in many respects this is true. Nonetheless, if the board understands the big decisions around data, platforms and systems of intelligence at a strategic level, and employs experts to help make the decisions at a micro level, then they will find themselves in an extremely strong position to help steer their organisation through a digital transformation.

With sound investment management, technology risk management and board alignment, you are well placed to accelerate change in your business.

And that brings us to the end of part III. In the conclusion, we share our final thoughts and advice on how you can capitalise on the digital opportunity.

CONCLUSION
A cornucopia of opportunity

All men's gains are the fruit of venturing.
Herodotus

The rate of innovation in the new economy has fundamentally shifted traditional business models, and the trajectory of this disruptive force is only set to continue, as big-tech companies and start-ups invest heavily in all things digital. Stranded in the middle of this tremendous shift are the old guard — those who have thrived by mastering traditional business growth tactics.

Some say pre-digital incumbents have lost the war, and that their most successful years are behind them. But where naysayers see declining margins as inevitable following imminent disruption, those who understand digital see a cornucopia of opportunity. Pre-digital incumbents have deeply embedded supply chains, unique and impressive in-house expertise and capabilities, vast networks, and a strong customer base and reputation. As things stand, these assets are under-utilised because pre-digital incumbent leaders instinctively focus on and invest in outdated business strategies. But now more than ever a shift is required, and time is of the essence. Those who wish to realise success in the new economy need to take action and, rather than worrying about protecting the status quo, proactively seek to disrupt themselves before a competitor takes the honours.

As technologists working in a pre-digital incumbent, we understand the challenges you face as the leader of such an organisation, and the associated feeling of being overwhelmed in the face of change and uncertainty. That's why we've provided you with a succinct framework for transitioning your company successfully from pre-digital to digital. We don't underestimate the monolithic task of digital transformation, but we have sought to make a clear case that opportunity exists whether you reach for it or not.

We trust that, having read *Chasing Digital* in its entirety, you will now appreciate the importance of each chapter, and the layered framework we have created to help you successfully lead your digital transformation and imagine new horizons. Your strategy, organisational design and culture are vital to building your flywheel, which is powered by the three key digital components — data, platforms and systems of intelligence. The accelerators of change will help facilitate your digital transformation, ensuring sound leadership from your board, proper risk management practices to protect your organisation, and the right investment mindset to drive longevity and growth in the face of uncertainty.

Like all big business decisions, a conversion of this magnitude must be driven from the top, but support has to come from all levels of the organisation. To thrive, your organisation will need a dogged and determined leader, someone who is willing to push themselves and their organisation well outside of their respective comfort zones.

Invest in the future

To have a future, you must invest in it.

The new economy is only just getting started, and there is a huge amount of uncertainty regarding the future. What we do know is that technology will play a massive role in solving the most complicated political, societal and environmental problems we face today. Data, platforms and systems of intelligence will be fundamental to this.

The internet is a global and open platform that feeds off data and is the backbone of our new economy. So how big is the opportunity from here? According to the World Economic Forum, four billion people on this planet still don't have access to the internet. Bringing four billion people online presents a huge amount of opportunity, not just in terms of new markets, but with regard to the advancement of our species.

As more people and ideas join this global platform, novel interactions will continue to evolve and the global web of connectivity will grow. We will also see a massive shift in power, as centralised institutions and platforms, such as banks and governments, lose influence and control. We will see developing nations transition into thriving economies, and watch decentralised platforms facilitate interactions between parties without the need for an intermediary.

Artificial intelligence will play an ever more pivotal role in the advancement of our society and economy. One fascinating example of AI in action is at the confluence of machine learning and blockchain technology. Work in this area is only just beginning, but the foundations now exist to enable machines and algorithms to buy, sell and negotiate with one another without the need for human intervention. This activity is achieved through harnessing the power of smart contracts, immutable and decentralised blockchain ledgers and self-learning algorithms that feed off vast data sets.

Automated, self-governing 'systems' are only now becoming possible and will continue to evolve as blockchain, advances in imagery technology, cloud computing and artificial intelligence matures. The processes and laws that govern how we do business will completely change as these types of systems become commonplace. Just how this will affect the future of business is hard to say. What we can confidently predict is that those who aspire to be successful in the future must seek to understand and embrace these technologies and the associated opportunities they present.

Embrace the chase

There are signs everywhere that a metamorphosis is afoot in the business world. Some refer to this as the fourth revolution, while others see the change as simply the start of a new economy based on information, data or network effects. Regardless of how people define these developments, change is here. The pace and timing of technology development poses many questions, with many answers undiscovered. For us, change is the greatest known unknown and the only real consistent force. Remember, there is no end to this transformation; you'll always be chasing digital.

Ambitious organisations must embrace the chase and establish the necessary digital foundations to meet new challenges as they present themselves. Businesses that cling to the status quo risk losing their competitive edge and, we believe, their viability. The internet has led to mass disruption as businesses of all shapes and sizes, in every industry and around the globe, race to develop strategies that enable new avenues of growth. *Chasing Digital* provides a guide to help companies overcome the inevitable hurdles and chart a course for future success.

We hope *Chasing Digital* gives you the confidence to invest further in innovation and technology, and compete globally for years to come, regardless of sector or industry. This book is about how to create a legacy, not only for yourself, but for those who succeed you. It's a question of when, not if. So look to new horizons, learn from your customers, don't be afraid to fail, and remember that digital is a continual chase. There is no endpoint.

Sources

The following is a list of all books and articles referenced in the text as well a selection of further reading.

Adhikari, S. 2017. Tech execs move up the ASX. *The Australian*.

Van Alstyne, M.W., Parker, G.G. and Choudary, S.P. 2016. Pipelines, platforms, and the new rules of strategy. *Harvard Business Review*, pp. 54–60, 62.

Andreessen, M. 2011. Why software is eating the world. *Wall Street Journal*.

Anthony, S.D., Gilbert, C.G. and Johnson, M.W. 2017. *Dual Transformation: How to Reposition Today's Business while Creating the Future*. Harvard Business Review Press.

Assis, C. 2017. Tesla surpasses Ford as stock zooms to record. *MarketWatch*.

Azhar, A. 2017. When Moore's Law met AI: Artificial intelligence and the future of computing. *Medium*.

Baghai, M. and Coley, S. 2000. *The Alchemy of Growth: Practical Insights for Building the Enduring Enterprise*. Basic Books.

Benaich, N. 2017. 6 areas of AI and machine learning to watch closely. *Medium*.

Bhattacharjee, D., Müller, L. and Roggendhofer, S. 2011. Leading and governing the customer-centric organization. The importance of organizational design and structure. McKinsey.

Billund 2006. Lego's turnaround: Picking up the pieces. *The Economist*.

Bradley, C., Dawson, A. and MacKellar, C. 2016. How incumbents become digital disruptors. McKinsey.

Bradley, J. et al. 2005. How digital disruption is redefining industries. Lausanne (Switzerland). IMD.

Buffett, W.E. 1996. Chairman's letter, 1995.

Buvat, J. et al. 2017. *The Digital Culture Challenge: Closing the Employee–Leadership Gap*, Capgemini Consulting.

Calastone 2017. Technologists under-represented in leadership positions.

Cameron, K.S. and Quinn, R.E. 2011. *Diagnosing and Changing Organizational Culture: Based on the Competing Values Framework*, John Wiley & Sons.

Capgemini Digital Transformation Institute 2017. *The Digital Culture Challenge: Closing the Employee–Leadership Gap*.

Cheredar, T. 2011. Airbnb competitor Wimdu scores $90M, *VentureBeat*.

Christensen, C., 1997. *The Innovator's Dilemma*. Harvard Business School Press.

Christensen, C.M., Anthony, S.D. and Roth, E.A. 2004. *Seeing What's Next: Using the Theories of Innovation to Predict Industry Change*. 1st edn. Harvard Business Review Press.

Columbus, L., 2017. Roundup of Cloud Computing Forecasts, 2017. *Forbes*.

Cong, L. and He, Z. 2017. Blockchain disruption and smart contracts. *Economics of Networks eJournal*.

Crespi, F. and Quatraro, F., eds. 2015. *The Economics of Knowledge, Innovation and Systemic Technology Policy*, Routledge.

Cronin, B., 2016. The dynamic forces shaping AI. O'Reilly Media.

Crozier, R. 2017. Macquarie Bank pilots open banking platform, *iTnews*.

Crunchbase 2017. Global Innovation Investment Report, USA. *Crunchbase*.

Deere, J. 2016. John Deere opens data platform to other software suppliers.

Deloitte 2013. Diversity's new frontier. *Deloitte Insights*.

Douetteau, F. 2017. Companies don't have a data problem, they have a data value problem. *Machine Learnings*.

Duggan, W. 2015. What does O2O mean for the future of e-commerce? *Yahoo! Finance*.

Equifax 2017. Equifax announces cybersecurity incident involving consumer information.

Evans, R. and Gao, J. 2016. DeepMind AI reduces Google data centre cooling bill by 40%. *DeepMind*.

EY Venture Capital Center of Excellence 2016. EY Global Venture Capital Trends 2015.

Fortune 2016. The 25 Best Global Companies to Work For. *Fortune*.

Fortune 2017. Google: #1 on 100 Best Companies to Work For in 2017. *Fortune*.

Frey, C.B. & Osborne, M.A. 2017. The future of employment: How susceptible are jobs to computerisation? *Technological Forecasting and Social Change* 114, pp. 254–80.

Furr, N. & Zhu, F. 2016. Transitioning your company from product to platform. *Harvard Business Review*.

Gall, J. & Blechman, R.O. 1977. *Systemantics: How Systems Work and Especially How They Fail*, Quadrangle.

Gallup 2017. State of the American Workplace.

Garcia-Alfaro, J. et al., eds. 2015. *Data Privacy Management, Autonomous Spontaneous Security, and Security Assurance illustrated*. Springer.

Gartner 2016. Gartner says by 2020, a corporate 'no-cloud' policy will be as rare as a 'no-internet' policy is today.

Gartner 2016. Gartner survey reveals investment in big data is up but fewer organizations plan to invest.

Gates, B., Myhrvold, N. and Rinearson, P. 1995. *The Road Ahead*, 1st edn, Viking.

Geertz, C. 1973. Thick description: Toward an interpretive theory of culture. From *The Interpretation of Cultures: Selected Essays*.

Geertz, C. 1973 (2008). *The Interpretation of Cultures: Selected Essays*. Basic Books.

Geissbauer, R., Vedsø, J. and Schrauf, S. 2016. *A Strategist's Guide to Industry 4.0*.

Glassdoor 2017. Glassdoor announces winners of its employees' choice awards recognizing the best places to work in 2018.

Gloster, S. 2017. Data breaches the looming drain on brand trust, *Australian Financial Review*.

Golden, J. 2017. Lessons learned scaling Airbnb 100X. *Medium*.

Greene, J. 2016. Microsoft to acquire LinkedIn for $26.2 billion. *Wall Street Journal*.

Greene, T. 2017. LinkedIn loses legal right to protect user data from AI scraping. *The Next Web*.

Gupta, L. 2015. Android — moat or economic castle. Should Google revisit its choice? *Medium*.

Hagstrom, R.G. 2013. *The Warren Buffett Way*, John Wiley & Sons.

Hardy, Q. 2015. IBM to acquire the Weather Company. *New York Times.*

IDC 2016. Worldwide big data and business analytics revenues forecast to reach $187 billion in 2019, according to IDC.

IDG 2016. 2016 IDG Enterprise Cloud Computing Survey.

Ignatius, A. and Bezos, J. 2013. Jeff Bezos on leading for the long-term at Amazon. *Harvard Business Review.*

Investopedia, Burn Rate.

Jacobs, M. 2017. Software licensing decisions: Consider dual licensing.

Jyoti, R. and Jezhkova, N. Worldwide Storage for Big Data and Analytics Forecast, 2017–2021. IDC.

Kessler, Z. 2016. Millennials. *Bloomberg View.*

Kharpal, A. 2017. China's ride-hailing giant Didi Chuxing raises $5.5 billion, valued at $50 billion. CNBC.

Kishigami, J. et al. 2015. The blockchain-based digital content distribution system. In 2015 IEEE Fifth International Conference on Big Data and Cloud Computing. (BDCloud). pp. 187–90.

Knight, W. 2016. The AI that cut Google's energy bill could soon help you. *MIT Technology Review.*

Konduru, V. 2017. 3 ways data quality impacts predictive analytics, towards data science. *Medium.*

Korn Ferry 2013. The digital board: Appointing non-executive directors for the internet economy.

Lavender, J., Hughes, B. and Speier, A. 2017. KPMG *Venture Pulse* Q3, 2017.

Loizos, C. 2017. As Uber's value slips on the secondary market, Lyft's is rising. *TechCrunch.*

Lovinus, A. 2016. Top CPUs 2016 best processors for business systems. *HardBoiled*.

Luxton, E., 2016. 4 billion people still don't have internet access. Here's how to connect them. World Economic Forum.

Lynley, M. 2017. The new iPhone 8 has a custom GPU designed by Apple with its new A11 Bionic chip. *TechCrunch*.

Manville, B. 2016. Are platform businesses eating the world? *Forbes*, 14 February.

Marr, B. 2014. Big Data: The 5 Vs everyone must know.

Marr, B. 2017. Data Strategy: *How to Profit from a World of Big Data, Analytics and the Internet of Things*. Kogan Page.

McAfee, A. and Brynjolfsson, E. 2017. *Machine, Platform, Crowd: Harnessing Our Digital Future*. W.W. Norton.

McChesney, C., Covey, S. and Huling, J. 2012. *The 4 Disciplines of Execution: Achieving Your Wildly Important Goals*. Simon and Schuster.

de Montcheuil, Y. 2015. IBM acquires the Weather Channel: when technology vendors become data vendors. *InfoWorld*.

Morgan, S. 2016. Cybercrime Damage Costs $6 Trillion in 2021. Market Data. *Cybersecurity Ventures*.

Mui, C. 2012. How Kodak failed. *Forbes*.

Nakamoto, S. 2009. Bitcoin: A peer-to-peer electronic cash system. bitcoin.org.

Newman, L.H. 2017. The Equifax breach was entirely preventable. *Wired*.

Ng, A. 2016. What AI can and can't do. *Harvard Business Review*.

Opensource.org, The open source definition (annotated). Open Source Initiative.

O'Reilly, G.M., Mori, A. and Cameron, P.A. 2003. Measuring the immeasurable. *Medical Journal of Australia* 179(1).

Parker, G. and Van Alstyne, M.W. 2017. Innovation, openness, and platform control. *Management Science.*

Parker, G.G., Van Alstyne, M.W. and Choudary, S.P. 2016. *Platform Revolution: How Networked Markets Are Transforming the Economy — and How to Make Them Work for You.* 1st edn. W.W. Norton.

Paul, K. 2017. Top 10 car manufacturers in the world in 2016. *DriveSpark.*

Ponemon Institute LLC 2017. Ponemon Institute's 2017 Cost of Data Breach Study: Australia.

Porter, M.E. 1997. *Michael Porter's Landmark Trilogy: Competitive Strategy/Competitive Advantage/Competitive Advantage of Nations.* Free Press.

Porter, M.E. 1998. *Competitive Strategy: Techniques for Analyzing Industries and Competitors.* Free Press.

Porter's five forces analysis, Wikipedia.

Rauser, A. 2016. *Digital Strategy: A Guide to Digital Business Transformation.* CreateSpace Independent Publishing Platform.

Ravichandran, D., Lu, J. and Lee, R., 2017. Airbnb vs Uber: Who will win the on-demand economy? *Fortune.*

Redman, T.C. 2008. *Data Driven: Profiting from Your Most Important Business Asset.* Harvard Business Press.

Reuters, 2017. Netflix's binge-watching model is set to take over TV. *Fortune.*

Reynolds, A. and Lewis, D. 2017. Teams solve problems faster when they're more cognitively diverse. *Harvard Business Review.*

Rickards, T. and Grossman, R. 2017. The board directors you need for a digital transformation. *Harvard Business Review*.

Rosic, A. 2016. What is Ethereum? A Step-by-Step Beginners Guide [Ultimate Guide]. *Blockgeeks*.

Ross, J. The fundamental flaw in AI implementation. *Sloan Review*.

Rowley, J.D. 2017. Q3 2017 Global Report: VC Deal and dollar volume projected to reach post-dot com highs. *Crunchbase News*.

Sadkowsky, T. 2017. How can thick data improve the way we use big data?

Sarrazin, H. 2016. Adapting your board to the digital age. McKinsey.

Schwab, Klaus 2016. The Fourth Industrial Revolution: What it means and how to respond. World Economic Forum.

Scott, K.M. 2017. *Radical Candor: Be a Kick-Ass Boss without Losing Your Humanity*. 1st edn. St. Martin's Press.

Seely, S. 2016. The Amazon Flywheel: Part 1. Sam Seely.

Shah, S. Transcript: @Chamath At StrictlyVC's Insider Series.

Shankar, R. 2017. Weaving your own big data fabric. *Dataversity*.

Shapiro, C. and Varian, H.R. 1999. *Information Rules: A Strategic Guide to the Network Economy*, Harvard Business Press.

Simonite, T. 2017. To compete with new rivals, chipmaker Nvidia shares its secrets. *WIRED*.

Smith, C. 2017. 125 Amazon statistics and facts. (November 2017). By the numbers.

Susskind, R. and Susskind, D. 2015. *The Future of the Professions: How Technology Will Transform the Work of Human Experts*, Oxford University Press.

The last Kodak moment? 2012. *The Economist*.

Thompson, B. 2015. Netflix and the conservation of attractive profits. *Stratechery*.

Thompson, B. 2016. Defining aggregators. *Stratechery*.

Thompson, B. 2017. Alexa: Amazon's operating system. *Stratechery*.

Thompson, B., 2017. Everything is changing; So should antitrust. *Stratechery*.

Thompson, C. 2013. Relying on algorithms and bots can be really, really dangerous. *Wired*.

Tung, L. 2016. From open-source hater to no. 1 fan: Microsoft now tops Google, Facebook in GitHub contributors. *ZDNet*.

Vermeulen, F. 2017. What so many strategists get wrong about digital disruption. *Harvard Business Review*.

Wang, T. 2013. Why big data needs thick data. Ethnography matters. *Medium*.

Wang, T. 2016. The cost of missing something. TEDxCambridge.

Wang, T. 2016. Why big data needs thick data. *Medium*.

Waters, R. 2013. Slimmed-down Kodak emerges from bankruptcy. *Financial Times*.

Westerman, G., Bonnet, D. and McAfee, A. 2014. *Leading Digital: Turning Technology into Business Transformation*, Harvard Business Press.

Wikipedia 2017. Robin Dunbar.

Index